WHAT OTHERS ARE SAYING

Savvy writers know if they want a book to sell, they must sell it themselves through store visits, signings, readings. In my leadership role in a large writers organization, I've seen countless writers flub appearances, and I've suffered through far too many disappointing readings. Every writer needs this book. It tells you how to sell yourself to sell your books.

Al Sampson, President, Seattle Institute of Media Arts

Melanie Workhoven is a wonderful teacher and a dynamic speaker. This book will help any writer give much better presentations.

Paul Lerner, author, LERNER'S CONSUMER GUIDE TO HEALTH CARE:
HOW TO GET THE BEST HEALTH CARE FOR LESS,
as seen on a 5-part series on NBC's "Today Show"

Peter Kahle has found the cure for the common reading. He knows how to make his own writing come alive when read aloud and now in "Naked at the Podium," he shares his secrets with his fellow writers. This is a must read for any author who wants to sell more books.

Gary Boynton, co-author, YOGA NUTRITION: A BALANCED PLAN FOR HEALTH,
LONGEVITY AND WELL-BEING, true-crime writer/teacher

I've worked with Melanie Workhoven for the past three years and know her to be an unusually talented, versatile actor. And, from my view (as an actor and public speaker) I can tell you that her advice to writers who want to speak convincingly and winningly to their public is right on the mark!

Peg Phillips, actor, Artistic Director/Founder, The Woodinville Repertory Theatre

All I ever needed to know about presenting myself and my material I could have learned from Melanie Workhoven. In partnership with the highly-regarded author, Peter Kahle, she now offers us the gift of her simple secrets in this eminently readable, entertaining book.

Evelyn McDaniel Gibb, author, TWO WHEELS NORTH: CYCLING THE WEST COAST IN 1909

I attended a writers' conference recently and took a class taught by Melanie Workhoven. Her presentation was so informative that it made the entire conference worthwhile for me. She gave me specific tips in my area of special interest, as well as reinforcing the things I was doing right.

Theresa Barker, Past President, Seattle Writer's Association

There are some key principles in reading live to an audience. These principles are not trade secrets…. It's always good to have reminders of these steps in order to let the words on the page reach the ear of the audience. What a good idea, now authors who read their works out loud can have just a little acting training to more effectively convey their works to a live audience

Hal Ryder, Professor of Acting, Cornish College of the Arts, Seattle, Washington, freelance director, CEO Educational Arts Resource Services, Inc./ ShakespearePlus

This is the only book of its kind available in the stores and it is marvelous. I am happy to champion it.

Bharti Kirchner, author of the novels, SHIVA DANCING and SHARMILA'S BOOK

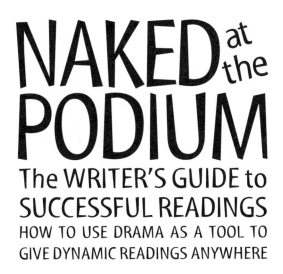

NAKED at the PODIUM

The WRITER'S GUIDE to SUCCESSFUL READINGS

HOW TO USE DRAMA AS A TOOL TO GIVE DYNAMIC READINGS ANYWHERE

Peter V. T. Kahle and Melanie Workhoven

74th Street Productions LLC

Seattle, Washington

NAKED AT THE PODIUM:
The Writer's Guide to Successful Readings

Copyright © 2001
Peter V. T. Kahle and Melanie Workhoven

Books by Seventy Fourth Street Productions
are available directly from the Publisher:

Seventy Fourth Street Productions LLC

350 North 74th Street
Seattle, Washington 98103
206-781-1447 PHONE/FAX
E-MAIL info@74thstreet.com
www.74thstreet.com / www.writersatthepodium.com

Graphic Production:
ART & DESIGN SERVICE, Seattle, Washington

Publisher's Cataloging-in-Publication

Kahle, Peter V. T.
    Naked at the podium : the writer's guide to
successful readings : how to use drama as a tool to give
dynamic readings anywhere / Peter V. T. Kahle and Melanie
Workhoven. -- 1st ed.
    p. cm.
    Includes bibliographical references.
    ISBN: 0-9655702-3-1

    1. Advertising--Books. 2. Public speaking.
3. Authors and readers. 4. Book talks. 5. Books--
Marketing. I. Workhoven, Melanie. II. Title.

Z278.K34 2001   659.1'9'002
                                 QBI01-200449
                                 2001 126047

FIRST EDITION
Printed and bound in Canada
05 04 03 02 01   1 2 3 4 5

To my wonderful students
who have taught me that when we trust ourselves,
all things are possible;
my son Matthew for his love and support,
and especially

to my father who was my best friend and inspiration.

Melanie

To George the Monkey —
where the hell's my yellow hat?!
And especially

to Lani who probably knows.

Peter

ABOUT THE AUTHORS

PETER V. T. KAHLE

Born in Seattle, Washington, he is a graduate of Michigan State University and studied writing at the University of Washington. He has been a teacher and stained glass artist. A past president of the Pacific Northwest Writers Association, he is the author of two books for children/young adults, *Shakespeare's A Midsummer Night's Dream: A Prose Narrative* and *Shakespeare's The Tempest: A Prose Narrative*. The books are re-tellings of the plays in story form and were finalists for the national *Small Press Book Awards* and *Independent Publisher Book Awards,* respectively. Mr. Kahle, a Shakespeare enthusiast, is a frequent speaker at schools and libraries on how to introduce children (and adults) to Shakespeare and the theatre, and also on presentation skills for writers.

MELANIE WORKHOVEN

Originally from the Midwest, she attended Northwestern University, majoring in Oral Interpretation. She studied improvisation at Paramount Studios, and voice with Mary Massey. She has been a radio personality, voiceover talent, copywriter, teacher and acting coach. Theatrical background includes the stage, major motion pictures and network television. Ms. Workhoven is a personal acting coach and conducts actor's workshops, as well as writer's workshops especially designed to teach drama and acting strategies to writers seeking to hone their presentation and public reading skills.

HOW TO CONTACT THE AUTHORS

Requests for information about scheduling workshops
or appearances should be directed to the authors through
74th Street Productions, 350 N. 74th Street, Seattle, Washington 98103.
PHONE/FAX 206-781-1447 / E-MAIL info@74thstreet.com

ACKNOWLEDGEMENTS

We are deeply indebted to the following people who have so kindly helped us in the preparation of this book.

For the stories we have used, for the quotes we have unearthed, we gleefully thank Marvin Bell, Evelyn Gibb, Nina Keali'iwahamana, Gary Larson, Larry McMurtry, Masafumi Nakane, Gordon Rapozo and his golf pants, Tom Robbins and Herb Tajalle.

For their dedication, candor and encouragement, we are grateful to the Seattle literary and theatrical community. We especially thank: Judith Chandler, Third Place Books; Mary Gleysteen, Eagle Harbor Book Store; John Marshall, Open Books A Poem Emporium; Christy McDanold, The Secret Garden Book Store; Gail Paul, Barnes & Noble Booksellers; Nancy Pearl, Washington Center for the Book; Peg Phillips, Woodinville Repertory Theatre; Hal Ryder, Cornish College of the Arts, and Albert Sampson.

For their unabridged comments and thoughtful suggestions, we cheerfully applaud the stalwart members of our critique group, Billee Escott, George Fleck, Lyn Macfarlane, Sheri Short, Cheryl Tsang and John Urbach.

Most important of all, we want to thank Lani Jacobsen and the amazing *Team Naked Ground Crew* at 74th Street Productions: Deb Figen, Jeff Jacobsen, Barbara Nickerson and Greg Nystrom who bravely took this whisper of an idea and made it happen.

SPECIAL ACKNOWLEDGEMENT

Luanne LaLonde

Chapter Eleven — *Audience Members with Disabilities*— was written by Luanne LaLonde, a former Microsoft product manager. Luanne was one of the principal members of Microsoft's Accessibility Technology Group, dedicated to improving software and computer access for people with disabilities. Her enthusiastic agreement to share her knowledge of this diverse community, and her depth of experience in speaking to this audience worldwide, help make this book valuable beyond measure. For her dedication to making the world better, for her wit and for her unselfish assistance in the making of this book, we sincerely thank her.

NAKED at the PODIUM:

The WRITER'S GUIDE to SUCCESSFUL READINGS

PREFACE

Would you take acting lessons if they would help you sell your books?

That's not as crazy as it sounds. The importance of doing readings and author appearances is a central theme in all the good books on marketing and self-promotion for writers. These books have lots of great information, but when it comes to preparing for a reading, most of it is organizational: invite every friend and connection you know, call the store in advance to be sure they have books on hand, and so forth. Fine, as far as it goes.

But what about the moment when you are alone with a microphone and your book? Everybody is waiting for you to say something. Your mouth is suddenly very dry. Is that your nightmare?

Then this book was written for you.

Most books on presentation skills are written either for actors or for business people. Writers need those skills, too, but the singular requirements for presenting books demand an approach adapted specifically for the purpose. Bringing together an acting coach and a writer as co-authors, this book addresses the writer's needs.

NAKED AT THE PODIUM is about creating your performer's persona, and enlarging selections from your book into pieces you can perform. There is a whole shelf of books (see *Bibliography,* page 155 for a sampling) that will tell you about advertising and marketing, and the specialized world of radio and TV skills. We're talking about building your basics: voice, repertoire and stage presence. You can't fire a cannon from a canoe. Build the foundation you need.

Each of us has written out of our own personal expertise, but the book itself is a blend of our voices. Individual first-person experiences are identified by our initials, like this:

> PK: I've done my share of readings and spoken in front of many groups, but before I went on tour with my second book I got a chance to work with Melanie. I thought, why not? Maybe she can teach me a trick or two. She did. In spades.
>
> "The first thing you need to do," she said, "is learn how to breathe." Silly me, I thought I knew how. She showed me what she meant after I read for her. "Your voice drops at the end of a phrase or sentence. That's normal in conversation. Actors know that you can only let it drop so far, or the audience will lose it. The secret is breath control, choosing when to take a breath so you have enough air for the final notes."
>
> Melanie taught me simple breathing exercises to get my voice warmed up and ready. Then we practiced the selections I was to read. For instance, this sentence:

"This is a tale of revenge and true love, about a wise magician, an angry monster, a grief-stricken king, a handsome prince, a beautiful maiden and two treacherous brothers."

"You need to break up that list," she said. "Pause after 'love,' breathe after 'monster' and 'maiden.' Use the pause to make eye contact."

Her advice was so helpful that I had a great time on my tour. Afterwards, I suggested to the Pacific Northwest Writers Association that she be asked to do a workshop at their summer conference. I have worked with PNWA for over a decade, helping writers learn to market their books. I thought that she offered something new.

MW: My workshop at the conference was a smash hit. Other groups and individuals sought out my services. I was amazed at how willing the authors seemed to be to participate and perform. I said to Pete, "They ask me questions about working with bookstores, and things I don't know about. What do I tell them? You know about this stuff better than I do."

And so this book was born.

CONTENTS

PHOTOGRAPHS

INTRODUCTION

I was born modest, but it wore off.

Mark Twain

If you want your book to sell, you must stand up in front of crowds of people and sell it. Are you ready?

Is your voice warmed up?

Can you do anything else besides read?

Published authors need two separate sets of skills. The first set is the creative/compulsive set, applying the writer's backside to the seat of the chair, creating the book. Writers either have this set in abundance, or they don't have a finished book to sell. The second set of skills is very different. We writers have to emerge from our caves and stand up in front of the people. We have to make them fall in love with our book and buy it.

Surveys consistently show most Americans have a fear of speaking in public. It's not surprising that many writers feel unprepared. Yet any book that hopes to find an audience needs an author as brazen as a carnival pitchman. With so much competition for free time and entertainment dollars, a single book is a candle in a universe of stars. Sales reps and promotions may move the goods, but only you, the writer, have the true believer's faith and focus on your book. Only you can do what has to be done.

Authors are everywhere these days, pitching their books — bookstores, yes, but also at libraries, on lecture series, in chat rooms and Web sites, on radio, and on every television interview show from local access cable to "Oprah". The result of this greater exposure is that audiences are expecting a greater level of performance. A reading is not just a reading, it's so much more it's almost a presentation. They want you to bring something extra to the event, some extra information, or connection. They want you to be comfortable, and fluent. You have to engage your audience.

The great majority of books on presentation skills are aimed at business people and designed for meetings. Most books on book promotion mention readings, but do not suggest how to construct one, or how to combat stage fright. Books on voice development and characterization are aimed at actors and don't say anything about closing the sale.

So how do you get prepared? What do you need to know?

Before you stand up in the front of the room,
you need to know how to:

Prepare for public speaking.

Design your presentation.

Rehearse your material.

Warm up for a performance.

When you get on stage, you need to know how to:

Read the room.

React if everything goes wrong.

Make the sale.

This book is the first that combines the experiences and skills of a stage, film and television actor, radio personality and acting coach with those of a published author with more than a decade of experience organizing writers conferences. And between us we've interviewed bookstore owners, librarians, writers, publicists and publishers to get their impressions.

The succeeding chapters will take you, by way of exercises, checklists and anecdotes, through the process of preparing yourself to give your book the presentation it deserves.

The body is the performer's instrument. We will discuss how to breathe properly for pitch and voice control, and how to build confidence before we go on stage.

Designing your presentation requires choosing reading selections to show off the best qualities of your book, with an eye to the demands of audience and venue. Can you do a demonstration or workshop, any kind of "song and dance" that can create extra value for your audience?

You will learn how to tailor your rehearsals toward the events as you schedule them. Once you've got your act together, you have to take it on the road. Unless you're Stephen King, you'll probably have to carry your own bags. Remember that road trip at Spring Break? With a little planning, this can be fun.

Rehearsal and exercises will help make you a more fluent advocate for your book. Exercises help you develop stage presence. You learn how to size up any space. Warming-up exercises show you how to place and support your voice, how to tune your instrument for the conditions: indoors or outdoors, lecture or intimate gathering.

We'll discuss how to have two heads when you arrive at a store or a hall for your appearance. You'll need one head to handle the business details and make sure that everything goes smoothly, and that your host remembers you fondly and invites you back. That leaves your other head free to prepare to perform.

So you were expecting the ladies quilting group and got the Harley-Davidson motorcycle club instead. An actor reads the audience, homing in on their reactions. Learn to shape your material on the fly to fit the group you've got; also what to do if the audience is deaf or hearing impaired, and you have a sign language interpreter. And what if NOBODY shows up? Disaster planning can help you salvage your morale — and make the bookstore staff love you anyway, and want to sell your books even after you've gone.

Finally, we'll talk about how to close the sale. This is almost as scary as public speaking, for most people. There is no magic wand to make this easy. But if you can engage your audience, if you can make them laugh, or cry, or learn something, you'll sell books. And they will remember you for next time.

So. You've written the greatest novel since *War and Peace.* Or was it the outstanding biography of Mother Theresa? Anyway, publishers fought for it, they're bringing it out without changing a comma. It's a writer's dream. Then one day you get a call from someone in the publisher's marketing department. "We're setting up an author's tour," she says. "What else can you do besides read?"

CHAPTER ONE

Preparation

The art of acting is the ability to do nothing.
Sir Alec Guinness

Why don't you try acting, dear boy.
It's so much easier.
Sir Laurence Olivier

Before we begin, know this: you have a marvelous advantage as a performer. You have already had success! Your book is published. People are reading it. They are curious about the author (that's you) and *they want to meet you!*

Meanwhile, you would very much like to be a strong voice for your book. To become an effective reader you must learn how to make the most of your physical equipment, and how to prepare for reading success the way an actor does.

If you've been to a reading by a favorite author, think back to that experience. If not, imagine getting to meet that author you so admire and hear him read from his own work. Imagine seeing her at a bookstore and being able to listen to her voice saying those spellbinding words.

Notice anything else about this experience? You don't expect your idol to be a brilliant actor, do you? As long as they're not too stick-like, it's okay. You just want the unforgettable experience of hearing this person reading from his or her own work. You *want to like* this person whom you have already admired from afar, so to speak. You are not there to be judgmental, but to be able to say, "I heard him read from his own work." "I was at her first book reading back before she became famous. I knew the moment I read that book it would be a huge success."

See? You're completely ready to be enchanted. This is a universal truth. Your readers have come to honor Caesar, not bury him. This is your edge — your secret weapon. Never forget that. People really do want to like you.

We have all heard the joke about the circus worker who complains about cleaning up after the elephants; but, when asked why he doesn't get another job, replies, "What, and give up show business?" At this point you may be wondering just how you got yourself into this fine mess. You are a writer. A private person happily alone with your muse or demon as the case may be, working away in complete isolation. You weave wondrous spells, tell outrageous tales, uplift and inspire protected by the walls of your sanctuary.

But if you want to enjoy optimum success as an author you're going to have to get out there and read and make presentations and even — gasp — perhaps an appearance on important late-night talk shows with Leno or Letterman. Believe it or not, you have more in common with actors than you think you do. You see, actors and writers are actually heads and tails of the same coin.

Barbra Streisand has always described herself as an actress who sings. She makes this distinction because for her, music has always been about communicating themes, ideas, feelings. As a writer, this is your focus too. Why do you write? To entertain, to inspire, to enlighten? Most artists who are compelled to create, aspire to illuminate their world. Even crazy comedian Jim Carrey was recently quoted as saying he wanted to be "a spirit of light in the universe."

The writer and the actor are driven by the same desire. While ideas funnel through your pen or keyboard, so to speak, those same ideas are played through the actor's voice and body. In the same way that the composer writes the music and the musician plays it, you create the music of words while the actor is the instrument through which those words and ideas are played.

So, let's get you ready.

As a writer doing readings you will need to use a highly complex, extremely sensitive communications tool — yourself! The exercises in this chapter will help you make the very most of your instrument, because the truth is, acting is extremely athletic. No matter what your age or size, no matter what your level of physical activity, the exercises that follow will increase vocal flexibility and range allowing you to be more expressive and more comfortable in front of a crowd. The simple body exercises will help increase your ability to express yourself naturally and effectively. You are about to learn how to bring your words to life.

Elongation

This first set of exercises will help unknot the body. Constricted, shortened muscles cause shaky hands, fluttering shaky voices, and knocking knees — don't laugh, it happens. The natural consequence of these conditions is performance anxiety. Note this: the biggest reason public speaking is frequently number one on the list of what most people fear, is because they don't know how to relax when speaking to groups. The second biggest reason is that they don't know how to breathe. It sounds strange, but wait, you're about to discover that you, yourself, may not have been really breathing all these years!

Elongation
Part One — CENTERED STANCE

1. Stand with your arms relaxed at sides and
    feet planted in a parallel line with your hips.

2. Relax.

3. Gently squeeze your belly button toward the
    back of your spine. *Feel your pelvis tip ever so
    slightly? If you are doing this right, you should
    feel your knees bend and relax just a little.*

4. Feel the balance in your body.
    You are now centered.

5. Notice your shoulders and your back.
    Do they feel tight? Mentally tell them to relax.

6. Breathe in *slowly.* Shoulders down, now!
    Use both your nose and your mouth to breathe in.
    Keep your mouth opening small, not wide;
    this will help use your nose.
    You should feel your rib cage expand
    up and away from your waist.

7. Now, *slowly exhale from your mouth only,*
    making an audible sound. It's good to make a
    "North Wind" face, with cheeks puffed out and
    lips pursed, to ensure you are really blowing
    the air out and not just letting it escape.

8. Repeat for four good breaths, fully drawing
    air in until you feel really full and your
    back rib cage area seems round and full.
    Blow each breath out slowly.

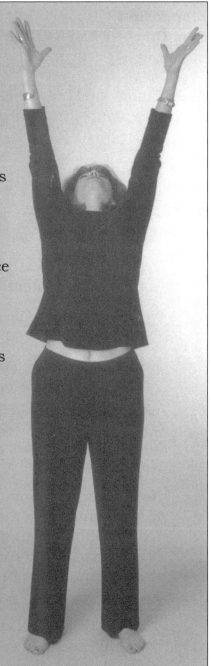

Elongation
Part Two —
UPWARD STRETCH

1. Breathe in, *using both your nose and your mouth;* slowly raise your arms above your head.

2. Breathe out *from the mouth only,* using your "North Wind" face as you reach up with your fingertips.

    Keep reaching, imagining your fingers are extending right through the ceiling.

    This process should be slow and steady.

3. Breathe in as you slowly bring your hands back down to your sides.

4. Repeat once.

Elongation
Part Three — DOWNWARD STRETCH

1. Mentally make your pelvis and legs a
   solid base. Breathe in slowly *nose and mouth;*
   gently let your torso "fall" with
   your arms dangling easily.

2. Breathe out *mouth only* and mentally push
   your fingers, hands, and
   wrists right through
   the floor.

   If you are
   limber, rest
   fingers or
   hands on
   the floor
   but imagine
   them going
   straight down
   through
   the floor.

3. Breathe in
   as you bend your
   knees and slowly
   curl back up into
   a centered
   standing position.

4. Repeat once.

Elongation
Part Four — SIDE STRETCH

1. From a centered stance, breath in
   nose and mouth, and raise your arms
   straight out
   from your sides,
   shoulder level.

2. Breathe out,

   remembering
   to blow out slowly.
   Isolate your upper body
   and elongate your arm,
   stretching to the right.

   Push your fingertips out,
   out, out, as though you
   were rubber like Gumby.

3. Breathe in, slowly
   returning to center
   and drop arms to sides.

4. Repeat the exercise
   stretching left, then
   returning to center position.

You should experience a feeling of overall well-being and relaxation after finishing these simple stretches. You may notice that you feel taller, more open and perhaps even a bit tingly from all the extra oxygen flowing into muscles that are now more relaxed.

Good! Now for something really strenuous, you get to lie down on the floor for...

Diaphragmatic Breathing

The purpose of this exercise is to show you what you've probably been missing all these years, when it comes to breathing. Many people breathe with their chests only, using just the upper lobes of the lungs. This leaves out about half their actual lung capacity and thereby increases their chances of feeling out of breath or shaky when trying to speak publicly.

A proper breath actually begins down below the rib cage in the diaphragm — the muscle that supports air as it is used for speaking and singing. Runners, dancers and other athletes commonly breathe up in the chest only, which works best for the kind of exertion they do. Actors, singers and speakers need to use diaphragmatic breathing in order to support the sound and have the breath for long sentences or long musical phrases.

The Straw exercise is done while lying on your back on the floor because that is the easiest way to actually feel what is working and how, without the distraction of other muscle groups getting in the way. This is also another great way to release tension, because when you lie down flat on the floor spread-eagle, the blood flows evenly throughout the body. As you breathe in fully, you are enriching the blood with oxygen. It reaches areas which may have had decreased blood flow due to tight, tense muscles. Here's where you learn to breathe.

Diaphragmatic Breathing
THE STRAW

1. Lie on the floor with your arms and legs comfortably apart from your body, spread-eagle fashion. Do not cross your feet or legs or curl your arms. You want to get an even distribution of blood and oxygen.

2. Place a large, heavy book on your midriff.

3. Mentally tell all your muscles to relax. Feel them spread out across the floor like melting ice cream.

4. Using one or both hands, place a real or imaginary straw to your lips and begin to suck air through the straw as you breathe in. Be sure to be aware of breathing with both your nose and your mouth.

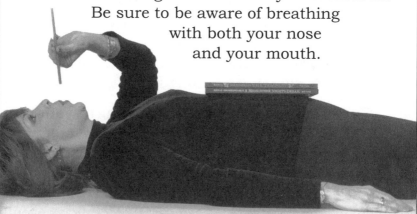

5. Notice how the book begins to rise from the *bottom* of your midriff first and *then* the top of the book comes up. The book helps you feel how your body takes in a full and complete breath, starting with the diaphragm. As you continue to breathe you will become more aware of the diaphragm *muscle* or *wall,* the support system for singing and public speaking. Continue inhaling until you feel your rib cage is almost to the bursting point.

6. Slowly begin counting out loud as the air releases. Keep your diaphragm taut so the sound is supported by as much air as possible and count, breathing out, until you are empty.

7. Repeat twice.

8. *Sit up slowly.* This is important because you have really oxygenated your body and you may feel a bit dizzy.

How do you feel? More open and relaxed, maybe even a bit refreshed?

Note: Most people can barely reach a count of twenty when they start but with practice you should be able to work your way up to a count of well above fifty. Counting should be steady and slow. Use 'one one-thousand, two one-thousand' if you like, at first, to get the right speed.

> MW: I recommend that performers do this breathing/relaxation technique before they leave for an appearance. Sitting on the floor, say something like, "How now brown cow," and notice the increased depth and resonance of your voice. You will probably hear quite a difference just from breathing correctly and relaxing your vocal equipment!

Vocal Placement

Now that you are breathing correctly, your next step is to make sure you have good vocal placement. Think of your head as your body's speaker system. Believe it or not, where you "place" the voice in your head, in your mouth and throat, makes all the difference in being able to fill a room without pushing or straining. Proper placement makes your voice sound richer, more pleasant, and more expressive. Singers speak of singing "in the mask," which means in the front of the face. Why? Because your sinus cavities are vibrating chambers for the voice. When you project sound into the sinuses, they become your very own amplifiers. We say people sound nasal when they have a cold, but actually being stuffed up takes away that vibrating chamber and what you hear is a lack of nasality — the human voice without amplification.

The following exercises will teach you to place the voice correctly for the fullest sound. This is also the way to avoid straining the voice or vocal exhaustion. Keep in mind that *you* hear your own voice while it is still inside your head, whereas your audience hears your voice once it is projected into the room. That is one reason why we think we sound different when we hear ourselves on tape.

Often people try to sing and speak in their throats because it sounds better to them, since the sound is close to their ears. Ever hear a concert where the male soloist was singing in the back of his throat? He probably thought it sounded great but we hear it as forced and rough.

This kind of sound does not carry well. It is trapped close to the performer's body and it takes a lot of vocal forcing to project it toward the audience. When sound is created in the mask, the full force of the sound is out in the room, not close to the performer's ear. So it is important in these next exercises to pay attention to how it *feels* to you, not how it *sounds* to you. You should feel an immediate difference when your vocal placement is correct. You should also notice more fullness and color in your voice. If you are the analytical type, tape-record these exercises and you'll hear the difference in your voice.

Do you remember Mama Dolls? When you tipped them forward, they would cry, "Ma-ma." Well, you are going to become a Mama Doll yourself in this exercise, and feel the power of proper vocal placement. It is the very best way to make sure you are correctly placing the voice in the mask easily and quickly. Here we go.

Vocal Placement
THE MAMA DOLL FLOP

1. Using your centered stance,
   imagine yourself a Mama Doll.
   Your legs and feet are a solid base.

2. Gently flop over from the waist and
   let your upper body dangle.

Make sure everything is completely
relaxed, except for your legs.

Let your arms dangle.
Keep your neck completely relaxed,
head falling naturally downward.

3. Breathe in slowly through
   the nose and the mouth.
   Notice how your torso pushes up
   and out as your diaphragm expands?

4. Keeping your head down and
   everything but your legs loose,
   say "MAMA, MAMA".

   You should feel the "M" sound
   creating a buzzing on your lips
   or nose, depending on how high
   or low your speaking voice is.
   This is the sound vibrating
   in the front of your face
   and it is your signal
   that YOU'VE GOT IT!

5. Repeat two or three times.

Vocal Placement
THE STANDING MAMA DOLL

1. Standing centered, evenly on both feet, breathe in using both nose and mouth.

2. Feel your spine supporting you and gently drop your head forward as you say, "Mama, Mama."

3. Repeat without dropping your head forward. Make sure you are still feeling the buzzing on your lips. If you do not feel at least a subtle vibration, go back to dropping the head down until you get the placement back.

"Mama, Mama."

Good work! Most students find that if they incorporate these exercises into their daily routine at least three times a week, it becomes second nature to breathe correctly when performing. Proper breathing and relaxed muscles create the confident, poised impression you, as a writer, want to present. An added bonus is the psychological edge it will give you to know that you are physically ready to perform and your voice and body will not sabotage you.

You also may find you've discovered a wonderful way to calm the jitters in other areas of your life. Just as women often find themselves doing their childbirth labor breathing at the dentist's office or when stuck in traffic, these stretch and breathing exercises are great coping skills for an amazing number of situations.

You'd never run in a marathon without training or play a musical instrument without tuning it, so you want to give the same thought and care to your personal communications equipment.

Now that you have learned the basics of keeping your instrument "in tune," it's time to think about designing your presentation.

CHAPTER TWO

Your Presentation

A little song, a little dance,
a little seltzer down your pants.

Chuckles the Clown

So, what else can you do besides read?

Word of mouth sells books. You need to give the people something to talk about. If you've written a book about snakes, bring a boa constrictor with you. You'd better warn your host about that. Some people are not snake-friendly.

The most important thing you can do with an audience is to engage the people, get some kind of emotional reaction out of them. You want them to empathize with you, and you want them to buy your book. That probably won't happen by accident. Plus, a good performance can energize the staff of a bookstore, and they'll be there to push your book every day of the week. Take advantage of this opportunity.

Even if it's just a sit-and-sign appearance, make the most of it. Bring something along to break the ice for potential customers. Something they can touch, a game they can play, a curiosity they can ask about. Be comfortable, dress for sitting down, and take good care of your hands. Customer attention will be focused on them as you autograph their copy. During intervals when the shop is quiet, talk to the sales staff; romance them; provide them with great one-liners to use to sell your book.

To prepare your presentation,
these are the steps you must take:

> Take a look at yourself and
> what you can bring to the party.
>
> Interview your STAR — your book.
>
> Determine what your audience wants.
>
> Spin your webs.
>
> Design your presentations —
> you'll need more than one.
>
> Size up the room.
>
> Get your act together.

Take a look at yourself

First things first: how comfortable are you about reading aloud and speaking on your feet? Exercises and rehearsal will help you. The whole point of rehearsal is to raise your comfort level on stage. What kind of settings and circumstances make you feel confident and in control? If a rabbit's foot helps, by all means keep one in your pocket.

> PK: I wear a string of good-luck beads under my shirt that I was given by the Zulu King's Lieutenant at Mardi Gras. Sure it's the twenty-first century, but if somebody wants to give me good luck, I'm not going to turn it down.

Think about what personal experience, training, competence or circumstance made you passionate enough to write your book. Your own personal story is usually of interest to your readers. How can you shape the telling of it to help them connect with you?

Do you possess any craft, skill or art related to the book that you could demonstrate? If you've written a book on quilting, show how to perform a certain stitch. If you love to make hand-dipped chocolates and so does the detective in your mystery, maybe you could make some right there in the store, or at least bring a few for your audience to taste. Create a shared experience with your audience.

One bookseller lamented, "If only novelists could do a slide show." What about it? Look for hooks in your story.

Can you conduct a short workshop or seminar based on your book? For example, if you've written a book on taxes, genealogy, punctuation, selling real estate, you could do something short and sharp that fits within your reading/appearance time slot. For a book on boat-building, bring a hands-on model.

Does your book exemplify a larger topic that you can speak about? If the hero of your novel is an abused child, can you talk on child abuse generally, or what caused you to take up the issue in your work?

Sadly, this is also the time to think about security. If you are writing about abortion, religion, terrorist groups, organized crime or some other high intensity subject, you need to think about your own personal security. It seems odd for a writer to worry about, but the extreme example of Salman Rushdie is still fresh. If your privacy is precious or likely to be threatened, take precautions. Use a post office box for correspondence, get an unlisted phone number, have people contact you through your publisher. This issue will come up again when we discuss sites and sightlines in Chapter Seven, but you should consider it early.

Interview your STAR — your book

Revisit your book with fresh eyes, and note the hot spots, the crucial episodes and/or concepts. What are the real grabbers? What does your editor think they are, or your agent, or any wise and trusted reader you can ask? Make a list.

Find several reading selections for each hot spot. Time your reading-out-loud speed. It's different for everybody, so determine your own. A rough rule of thumb would be 130–140 words per minute. If you rush, you garble your words; if you drag, you're a sleeping pill. Ask a friend, spouse or colleague to listen to you and report back. Tell them to be objective and even brutal, if need be.

The length of your selections is important. Appearances may range from fifteen minutes to an hour and a half. Given the informal nature of many book readings, you should choose several shorter passages instead of one or two long ones. That way, an audience member can listen to you read for five minutes or so and then move on if they have to. As a general rule, it is better to have three five-minute passages than one fifteen-minute section *unless you are in an intimate and fairly private setting where you don't expect your audience to come and go.* And choose sections you most enjoy reading. There's nothing more infectious than the performer's own enthusiasm.

Strive for a whole incident, description, concept or conversation; a selection shouldn't feel like a fragment. Sometimes you may have to trim the opening for the sake of length, but that's okay. Make them laugh, make them cry, make them learn something. These are the *tastes* that will sell your book.

Plan how to introduce your book smoothly. Lead your listeners right to the point where the reading selection picks up. Write a short introduction for each selection. Then take just the essential points and characters, and create a set of points short enough to fit on a sticky pad. Post the note on the page where the selection begins. Reading the introduction would feel too stiff. The notes allow you to simply tell it, with a guide to make sure you cover enough information to place your audience in the scene. Starting to read, getting three sentences in and having to stop to explain something is not good. Comedians call it 'stepping on your material.'

Determine what your audience wants

Poetry, Children's, Nonfiction: the audience for each field is different and distinct, and must be approached in its own fashion. You know the readers you wrote for, but within that field your audience may vary as well from appearance to appearance. What do they want and how best can you reach them?

For instance, let's say you have written a children's book and expect many parents and some children at your readings. You'll want to choose passages that you can bring to life vividly to keep the children entertained; you know, something with colorful characters you can act out and probably some moments of high drama, silliness or humor. Louder, more boisterous or dramatic passages are also good for an adult book if you know you will be reading in a high-traffic area. You have an excuse to raise your energy level, which not only helps your loyal readers huddled around you, but also helps draw in people who then become readers. For quieter settings you can choose more reflective selections.

Is there a special passage your audience expects to hear? Poets often have a particular poem that has to be part of every performance. If Marvin Bell doesn't read "To Dorothy," the program will feel incomplete.

Give the people what they want. Be hard-nosed and practical. Your goal is to intrigue and enchant. Your planned passage may not be the best choice for this presentation. Think like a producer, not like a critic!

Spin your webs

See how many webs you can invent for yourself. What are other authors doing in their appearances? Read the paper for the literary listings. Go to bookstores and libraries; watch and listen. If you can, ask staff members what works in their store. Check out the many titles available now on marketing your book, making sure you've got the up-to-date editions. Study the performance styles and skills of various types of TV personalities. Then hold a brainstorming session with a creative friend or two.

Think about ways you can enhance or set the stage for your presentation. Can you use any visual aids — art, posters, video, slides, flowers, a bust of Shakespeare? Is there any way to use music as part of your program? Ridley Pearson has written a series of books featuring a detective hero named Lou Boldt who likes to play jazz piano. For an appearance at Third Place Books in the Seattle area, a jazz musician friend of Pearson's organized the Lou Boldt Quartet. The quartet played a set, Pearson did his presentation, and then they played another set while he autographed books. Now that's friendship. And what a show for the customers!

If you're going to do a demonstration, focus on the details early. Make a list and check it twice; give yourself enough time to track down needed items well before Old Devil Stress sets in. You need to plan your wardrobe anyway, is there some sort of costume that would help set the tone? And we mean help, not hurt.

As an example of a brainstorming session, suppose you have written a nonfiction book about two boys riding their bicycles from California to Seattle, Washington in 1909. The book includes postcards and photographs from the trip and is based on letters and notes of one of the participants. Your market analysis suggests that your book will appeal to bicycle nuts, history buffs and kids anxious for adventure. Your book's hot spots are some dramatic riding incidents, your hero's presence at certain historic places and events, and human-interest incidents which demonstrate the society of the time and the character of the boys. You are a grandmotherly person whose only voice training is two generations of bedtime stories. Your brainstorm session might go something like this.

Bicycle Nuts

Which selections would be the most interesting for bike nuts? What pictures do I have of the actual bicycles the boys rode? Can I enlarge and mount them on foam core boards? What brand of bikes did the boys use? Is the company still in business? Do they have posters, photos, models, anything I can use for visual display? Bicycle stores, bike clubs — is there a bicycle history organization? A museum? Where else can I look for support materials? Is there a local bicycle celebrity? Can I arrange a joint appearance? Does anyone in town have antique bicycles? Would they come and bring one for an appearance? What about a scale model bicycle?

History Buffs

Which selections would be the most interesting for history buffs? How many local and state museums and historical societies are located along the route the boys traveled? Can I talk about the time period in which the adventure occurred? Are the newspapers that sponsored the trip still publishing? What did the boys carry with them — small, simple domestic artifacts that I can find from that period? Look for things that are out of use and quaint now, reflective of the change in times.

Kids Anxious for Adventure

Which selections would be most attractive to high school kids? Middle school kids? Riding bikes, animals, bold adventurous sequences — keep them short and punchy. Which visual aids would fit those selections? Use pictures of the bikes, and the things they carried. Which episodes talk about traveling, homesickness, and kids restless for adventure? Use the show and tell approach.

Besides being a terrific writer, Sherman Alexie is a great comedian, so he does a standup act and rarely reads much from his books. But by the time he's done with you, you want to read them. Now that's spinning a web!

Design your presentation

Using your book's hot spots, shape a presentation for each of your major audience types. You want to emerge from your brainstorming session with more reading selections than you can possibly do in a single appearance, more enhancements than you could carry in a pickup truck. Again, think like a producer, not a critic! So if your planned passage isn't the best choice when you see who's in the seats, no need to panic. You've got plenty of extra pieces prepared.

It may help to visualize each presentation as a pegboard with different shaped holes. You need a round peg to introduce yourself to the audience, a square one to introduce your book, two or three triangular pegs to romance the audience a bit, and a star-shaped one to close the sale. You want to have a selection of each shape of peg in your pocket so you can pick the perfect fit for each situation.

Program enhancements

It's important to evaluate your program enhancements. They should:

Have a real purpose.

Be easy to interpret. Aids lacking in clarity can confuse and annoy the audience.

Be displayed only one at a time, in general, unless the others are posters of various books you have written. Each visual aid should be visible by the entire audience.

Coordinate with your words. If you have poster-sized illustrations from a children's book, for example, don't talk about the barnyard while you're still showing the farmer's house.

Not distract. Handout material should be distributed at the end of your presentation. This prevents paper rustling and listeners from reading while you are speaking.

And remember, when using program enhancements, it's important to maintain eye contact with your audience. Talk to your listeners, not to the gimmick you're showing them.

Think big and then scale back. As much as possible, be self-contained. Remember you have to carry it, or depend on someone else to have the hardware you need to go on. Even if you call ahead to make arrangements, you don't want to fly twelve hundred miles to find out they don't have a carousel for your slides. Murphy's Law takes no holidays.

At the very minimum, carry a copy of your book. Always carry a copy of your book. Always, *always* carry a copy of your book. They're still laughing at the author who showed up for a radio interview and didn't have a copy with her. She said to the interviewer, "But I thought you'd have one." That thud you hear is the sound of opportunity walking into a door that should have been open.

Size up the room

The more you know about where you will be performing, the better prepared you will feel. The more prepared you feel, the more comfortable you will be. The more comfortable you are, the more creative you are. The more creative you are, the more fun you will have performing. And believe it or not, the more fun you have, the more successful you will be. This is one of the great mystic secrets all performers know. Now it is one of your secrets, too.

If you've never been to the location where you are scheduled to perform, plan a scouting expedition. If it is not possible to visit prior to your appearance, arrive early the day of your performance so you can get a feel for the space and make any necessary changes before you have to get up there and do your thing. Musicians do at least a mini-rehearsal in any hall where they will appear. Actors almost always rehearse on the stage where they will perform. Being familiar with your working area eliminates the need to adjust or compensate for unexpected conditions while you are performing. You don't want your concentration broken, that can lead to disasters.

Best option of all: visit the location when another author is doing a reading. Watching someone else reading may give you some great ideas for your own performance. You can see what works well and what is less successful.

It may seem obvious, but make sure you get answers in advance to the following questions.

Location:

Will you be appearing indoors or outside?

How big is the room you will be in?

Will it be a "closed" situation, or will people be coming and going as you are performing, such as an open area of a bookstore?

Is there a seating area?

Is there any kind of stage or platform?

How much distance will there be between you and the audience?

Does the area require a sound system?

What kind of peripheral noise should you expect?

How have other authors used the space?

What has been successful there in the past?

Type of function:

What time of day is your presentation? How might this affect your audience?

What sort of audience does your host expect? Is it a party, a fund-raiser, or other social gathering?

Will people be eating or drinking while you perform?

How many people are expected?

Are you the only scheduled performer?

How long are you expected to read?

After your reading, what other activities would your host like you to be involved in (i.e., book signing, Q & A period)?

You can see already how useful this information will be. An experienced performer can adjust to the unexpected, but, especially in the beginning, you want as few surprises as possible. You'll use some of this information right away, some of it you'll save for later, but the time to gather intelligence is now.

If you are not the only author on the program, you will have to shorten and sharpen your presentation. Do some quick Internet or bookstore research and find out about the other authors and their books. The audience will be a blend of people focused on different books. What is your most powerful selection for the audience you see before you? Cut to the chase.

Even a good surprise can throw you off and fracture your performance concentration. If you expect the press at your reading, it doesn't really change anything you do, but knowing it ahead of time will keep you from being taken off guard when you arrive. If the bookstore, publisher or your host has contacted the media, make sure they let you know before you are introduced whether any of the press are in the audience, and who they are.

Another consideration would be the taking of photographs or filming. You should discuss this with your host before the event as well. If it is desirable for you, arrange for it to be done in the most unobtrusive way possible. Your first obligation should be to your audience. Remember, audience members are your ambassadors! They are going to spread the word about your book.

Okay, let's look at some possible scenarios and how they might change what you plan to do. Let's say you have been asked to read outside at a country club or, what the heck, at the Hollywood Bowl. If the seating area is large or you expect outside noises or even steady background noise such as in a shopping mall, you'll want to make sure your host will be able to provide a microphone for you. There's nothing more defeating than knowing as you try to perform that half your audience can't even hear you. (We'll talk more about outdoor venues and microphones in subsequent chapters.)

On the other hand, if the room is very small and the crowd large, you may want to plan a shorter reading or perhaps plan several smaller readings. The host can advertise that you will be appearing at 11:30, 12:00, and 2:00 for example, with limited seating for each reading. In very intimate settings it is better not to use a mike. The warm, personal feeling possible in a small room can be destroyed with a mike and make you seem too formal.

Know everything you can about what it will be like when you do your reading, and your comfort level will translate to the audience. Even less than desirable circumstances can be joked about with them. If you aren't thrown, often times unplanned distractions can be an experience you've shared with your audience and become part of a special memory for them.

Now that you have designed your presentation and know what to prepare for, it's time for rehearsal techniques. As the actors say, let's get this show on its feet.

CHAPTER THREE

Your Cast of Characters

We just don't see you as bald.

Los Angeles casting director

Suppose you're a burly guy with a full beard, and you need to read the part of your frightened, dainty heroine. How do you keep from looking like a freak? You learn to read in character.

Remember the phrase, "Build it and they will come?" If you truly build your characters (following the simple guidelines in this book), your audience will come with you and follow the journey your characters take. The idea is to cast the same spell with your face, voice and body that you have with your pen or keyboard.

First, a simple truth about audiences, and this is a biggie. *They don't know what they want until <u>you</u> tell them.*

How many times have you read a book and imagined what the hero looked like? Then you hear about the movie star signed to play the film role and you think,

"No way…he's not what I imagined, he's all wrong for that part." But often, when you do see the film, the actor is so convincing you can no longer think of any other actor doing the role. Ann Rice was furious that Tom Cruise had been cast as her vampire until she saw the film and was thrilled with his work. And look at all the movie classics where the leading lady or leading man was not the studio's first choice. Then the film goes on to achieve legendary status and becomes a defining element of that actor's work. Here is a case in point.

An eager, up-and-coming actor went in to read for a nice-sized role in a television pilot. Entering the casting office, the actor quickly realized that several of the show's writers were sitting in on the auditions. This was a great opportunity for the actor to sell himself. He did his reading and was thrilled to hear appreciative laughter. The director praised his work, commenting on his comedy timing, his great look and how much they enjoyed the way he was bringing the script to life. But sadly, the director went on to explain the part called for a bald man. The actor could not believe his luck or how well his toupee was evidently working. He begged the Hollywoods to give him three minutes in order to show them something important.

He raced down the hall to the men's room and quickly removed his piece, washed the top of his blessedly bald head. Barreling back into the casting office, he spread his arms out with a TA-DA! smile, sure he'd nailed the job. There was a pause. Then, after glancing at his associates, the director proclaimed, "No, we just don't see you as bald."

The actor had done such a fabulous job of presenting his charming, funny persona-with-a-full-head-of-hair that he didn't seem believable as the talented bald guy he truly was. Talk about the magic of truthfully investing in your performance.

The take-home point is that your outer shell can still reflect a world of people and emotion IF YOU BELIEVE IT CAN. Build it and they will come. So, here's how to build it.

Character study

Wow, are you lucky! How many times have actors longed for the chance to ask the author what he/she meant, or what happened in what we actors call the "backstory" to make a character feel or act the way they do? Some authors give us a lot. Then there are authors like Shakespeare who make it a true collaboration with the actor. They just write about where the character is now and it's up to the actor to figure out how the character came to that mental and physical place. But you, the author, already know. Yet another advantage you have over the common garden-variety actor.

Now let's say you've written a nonfiction book about gardening, or deep-sea fishing or your adventures living in the Canadian wilderness. In each case, you are the character. Believe it or not, presenting yourself is often the most difficult acting job of all. One can get the feeling of being terribly exposed. Even professional performers can appear awkward when they are out of character.

Think about favorite actors you've seen on the "Tonight Show," for example. Some have a witty talk show personality. But others, who are so poised and powerful when they are playing a character, appear downright dull, dull, dull sitting there trying to talk to Jay Leno.

Presenting the character of *you* can be tricky indeed. Unless you are a natural ham or have a kind of droll persona you use at parties, the best way to develop your "character" for readings is to focus on the material you're presenting and let the subject matter become the character.

If your book is a personal recounting of events — say, your Canadian wilderness adventure — then your focus is on sharing and telling your story. Imagine that each person in the audience is a close friend and you can't wait to tell them what happened to you. Especially in humorous accounts, or extremely dramatic accounts such as Jon Krakauer's *Into Thin Air,* the author's perception of the events and reaction to them also becomes a part of the character.

If your nonfiction book is a biography, or features some strong personality, proceed to develop that character. If it is an examination of U.S.-Japanese relations during the Reagan Administration, bring out the dominant events and players. There is always some hook to hang your presentation on. Think of yourself as a visual aid to your material. Let that idea guide your choice of wardrobe and props. Then, get out of your own way and do not allow yourself to worry about any perceptions of you. Focus on creating positive impressions of your book.

Character preparation notes

Even though you've written the book and you know your characters, the following exercise will help you discover ways to physicalize aspects of the characters as you do your reading. Try to choose scenes with no more than two or three characters. One character is just fine, too, or one character reacting to a crowd. The objective is to have only a few dominant participants in your scene. Write down all the characters appearing in the scenes you will be reading and chart the following information about each one:

> What does this character want us/
> the other characters to know?
>
> What does this character want to hide?
>
> What does this character want to
> accomplish at this moment in the story?
>
> How does the character feel about what he/
> she is trying to accomplish?
>
> How is this character like you?
>
> How is this character different from you?
>
> How does this character feel about the other
> characters in the scene or scenes you are
> reading?
>
> How does the character feel about where he/
> she is headed?

These notes will provide a condensed reminder of the characters to help you rehearse.

If you only have one character in your reading, you will still want to answer the questions, but add how your character feels about people he *may* meet, *wants* to meet, or *has* met. Writing down these details about the characters' inner selves and perhaps a bit of their backstories, will help remind you of what emotions they are feeling — specifically the ones they want to hide and the ones they want to express.

You, as a writer, are fully aware of the layers that make up the human personality. Good actors must build some of these complex layers into their consciousness when they play a part or the character can seem pasted on. The great Meryl Streep always chooses a secret about each character she plays and won't reveal it to anyone until she is no longer playing the role. She believes her secret creates an added dimension making her character more interesting to watch. Few can argue with her success. If you like, pick a secret for each of your characters and add it to your character preparation notes. Even though you won't consciously be thinking about any of this back material while you read, it's important to have it there. Think of it as something you have to load onto your computer before you can run a program or play a game.

This brings us to another great truth about acting: *it's all in your head.* Now, if you get out of your own way and invest in your character mentally, it will magically transform your body, your voice, your face — your whole essence.

Here's a tip for getting in touch with your characters so that they will feel more comfortable inside you. Most actors work either from the outside in, or from the inside out. Some actors take a mental CD of character information and load it in their cranial hard drive. Then, suspending disbelief, they practice out loud and begin to find gestures, a way of walking, a tilting of the head that feels like the character. The mental leads to physical manifestations so they're working from the inside out. Other actors find a physical element that symbolizes for them a vital essence of the character. This leads them inward to tap the character mentally. There's no right or wrong here, just what works for you.

> MW: I usually work from the inside out, but when I was in my twenties, I was hired to play Elinor in "The Lion in Winter." Elinor was in her seventies, but she was also a queen. How could I, a young woman, somehow express her age physically and feel it internally in order to bring truth to the role? I certainly couldn't dodder about the stage because she was a queen with royal bearing. For several days I watched elderly people on the bus, walking down the street, wherever I was. Then one day in rehearsal, it came to me. I gave Elinor a tremor in her left hand. A slight palsy that became worse when she was upset. It was the magic key. Elinor and I formed a bond.
>
> To be sure, the makeup on my face helped the audience to visualize the aged woman I was creating. But that wouldn't have worked if I hadn't been mentally in her royal shoes and able to subtly communicate

her years to the audience in some physical way. I could then quickly and surely suspend my disbelief and *become* a woman who lived hundreds of years ago and with whom I had very little in common. Interestingly, giving my character the palsy helped me: I wasn't *playing* having the palsy. I was *playing trying not to have the palsy;* I was *playing trying to make it less obvious.* I felt I understood her pain and her passion. I felt her dignity and her exhaustion. In addition, the tremor in her hand helped me find a slight vocal tremor. Not enough to get in the way of her wonderfully poetic speeches, but just enough to suggest her age.

It turned out to be a very successful production. After the show, members of the audience would wait for the cast to come out and sign programs. I was thrilled to see how many people were actually shocked to meet me and realize how young I was.

Build it and they will come. Finding the right keys to your characters is essential and very rewarding. It's like finding your seat on a horse, being on your game, in your groove. And it is also the place from which you will feel the most confidence and freedom as you perform.

Character keys

To help you find keys to expressing your characters allow yourself to play with physical and mental ideas for each character.

Ask yourself what your character leads with — his head? Her heart? Does he stand slightly stooped? Is she extremely timid? Would she keep her head tilted down slightly as if protecting herself?

Determine how your character gestures. Big bold sweeping moves, or would they be off-handed? Find one or two key gestures and vocal characteristics that seem the most expressive of your character and let the rest go. You don't want to appear too busy. Especially if you are doing more than one character, a couple of distinctive gestures or vocal mannerisms will help your audience keep the character straight. Too many bits of business will make you look like you have fleas.

Establish what kind of voice your character has. You probably did this mentally while writing about the characters in your book, but now you want to take it another step. How are the voice tones, strong and rich? Nasal? Does he speak harshly? Does she hesitate slightly when nervous? Does he have a tendency to rush (not too much!) or sigh before saying something very private? Use these tricks sparingly for maximum effect.

You can actually create emotions in yourself by causing the physical changes that occur when these emotions exist. For example, if you clench your stomach, tighten your jaw, stiffen your chest and hold your breath for a moment and then breathe in quick shallow breaths, you will feel something very akin to anger. If you push your diaphragm down on your stomach, drop your shoulders, cast your eyes down and purse your lips, you will feel sad; maybe even feel your chin tremble and have the urge to cry. Try it and see.

You can also lift your diaphragm out of your waist, take a big breath, raise your eyes upward and feel a lightness very similar to joy. These are rather fun techniques to practice as they apply to your characters. Put yourself into the physical state of the character and often times it will help connect you to the scene. The techniques can also be helpful if you are feeling a bit of nerves when you stand up to perform.

Once you've made some decisions, add this information also to your character preparation notes. When you take these notes to rehearsal in the next chapter, you'll see how easy it is to become the bald man that Hollywood wanted.

CHAPTER FOUR

Getting Naked in Rehearsal

Is there a nude scene?

Eve, Garden of Eden

Rehearsal for many actors is an exciting time because it's all about experimentation and discovery. This is the time when you can play and give yourself the freedom to try anything. And best of all, the more fun you have, the more creative you become.

> MW: I cannot tell you anything more profound about acting than this: *the audience won't believe it unless you do.* A convincing performance starts with you and your willingness to let go and trust yourself. Will you get naked at the podium?

Create a mock performance site in your rehearsal space. Practice your character's voice and moves at a makeshift podium or holding the book on your lap the way you plan to use it at the reading. This will help you see what works and what feels awkward.

Rehearsing

MW: My advice is, unless you're a seasoned performer, don't try to memorize your reading. First, if you aren't used to the discipline of lengthy memorization it will be the death of you.

Second, I'm positive that reading and reciting memorized text are handled by different sections of the brain. I've developed this theory watching acting students try to recite memorized material while holding a script in front of them.

My experience suggests that looking at the written material breaks a certain stream of concentration. In practical terms, what tends to happen is that the actor has now lost his place in his head, and in seconds has also lost his place on the page and can't remember the script. It's like a huge metal wall has sealed off his functioning brain. The big blank-o. It is not a pretty sight. So my rule is memorize or read, don't try to do both.

And just to set the record absolutely straight with no possibility of doubt: when we talk about rehearsing and practicing, we mean *OUT LOUD.*

Not only do you need the practice, there is a brain connection thing going on here. Even actors cannot be fully convincing with material they have not practiced aloud over and over.

Eye contact

The real point of eye contact is to let the audience see you and empathize with you. As you practice and become extremely familiar with your script, you will want to find natural places to make eye contact with the audience.

Many actors like to use the energy they get from direct eye contact. Try this with a small group of family or friends and get the feel of it. If you can get that energy, it's a great boost.

But what if you're one of those people who find looking right into someone's eyes to be disconcerting? And it's not always the big hall full of people that's hard to face. Small gatherings can feel too personal or, as one actress described it, too naked. When you are up on a stage the audience is further away and usually in a darkened room so it's easy to look right at the audience — you can't really see them anyway.

Here's an effective trick that's almost impossible to detect; some actors prefer to use it when working a smaller, more intimate room. Look just slightly above the eyes. You will still see the person's eyes, but your sharp focus will be on their eyebrows or forehead. This is much less personal and disconcerting. An audience sitting three or four feet away cannot tell the difference.

This is a very good technique for anyone uncomfortable speaking in front of groups because it gives you a certain distance, helps you keep your concentration focused and still gives the audience the feeling that you are connecting with them.

However you handle this is fine. The important thing is to find a style that makes you comfortable.

It is a good rule of thumb to begin or end a thought or major point with eye contact. As you work with your text, you'll want to note important moments where eye contact will be especially effective. You might like to take the performance copy of your material and stick a marker by each of the places in your reading where you want to look up. Try them out. Decide on those key look-up moments, the ones you want to keep. Pull the extraneous markers.

And speaking of the rule of thumb, whenever you look up, keep your thumb next to your place. It will guide your eyes right back to the proper word without a stumble.

Some examples of eye contact moments:

If your grandmotherly sleuth is about to name the murderer, for example, you might read, "and once I realized that Lord Atherdon had never gone into the garden, I knew immediately that the murderer **(looking up at the audience)** *had to be none other than you, Miss Whartwimple!"*

Or, **(reading)** "...but the shadow over the moon seemed to cast a shadow on my heart and I wondered briefly **(looking up)** *is he never coming back to me?"*

Or, **(out to the audience)** "Richards was a fool-hardy man **(reading)** but his great wealth seemed never to run out. It was after some years of extreme excess that **(looking back up)** *the authorities began to ask why."*

This is the heart of your rehearsal. Delivering your book smoothly, while connecting with the audience is your ultimate goal.

Pitch and pacing

Variety in pitch and pacing is what puts color and life into your voice. Speaking on one note and with unvarying speed is deadly, for it becomes unbearably monotonous. You want to connect with your listeners, not put them in a coma.

Have you ever sung a song that was too high for you, or too low? You can't get any volume or control of the sound. Your speaking voice is normally set somewhere in mid-range, so you can go higher or lower at need, and still have voice control.

Refer to your character preparation notes to create a separate voice for each character in your first selection. Make sure each voice is within your comfortable vocal range, but give each one a slightly different sound. *Just a subtle difference,* that's all you need.

You may feel like you're back playing with dolls, or action figures, or stuffed animals, but you had the right idea when you were a kid. The voices made the characters feel more real to you, the kid playing. And they'll make the characters feel more real to you, the author reading, and to your audience. Create a voice for nonfiction and third-person narration, too. Try out various voices. *Experiment!*

Watch your reading speed. If you go faster you are implying excitement, enthusiasm, or fear. Slowing down conveys emphasis, solemnity or the voice of authority. Choose your speed on purpose, not by accident. Take full breaths, they'll help keep you calm and in tempo.

Be comfortable with silence. Allow yourself to pause. A pause is not a hesitation; a hesitation is a stumble, a pause is a planned effect. A pause is used for emphasis, to mark a sudden break of thought or action, and to test audience reaction. When your character says, "I never meant to tell you but — he is my son," you read it aloud with a pause where the dash is. That pause is there for dramatic effect. It indicates mental anguish on the part of the character, and allows the audience to have a moment of anticipation.

Sometimes the pause is for comic effect, or to let the laughter die away before you continue. In any event, the pause is your ally. Use it to take a full breath and gather yourself. If you find yourself hesitating, turn it into a pause, and let them believe you are reflecting. Don't fill space with an 'er' or an 'um'. That makes you sound like you're stuck. You may well be, but you don't want it to show.

Don't speak until you're ready. Always take a full breath before you launch yourself.

The performance copy

Your performance copy of your book can be your best friend. Tell it all your secrets, and it will remind you of them at the proper time.

Use the same text to rehearse and to perform. Don't practice with loose sheets and then do your reading with a book, for example. Your eyes get used to the look of the page and where each section of text is. The feel of the paper, the location of each printed word — you would be amazed how all of that is recorded by the brain. Then, when you perform, a part of your mind tracks it all. If your eye sees different placement it sends a kind of alert to the performer part of the brain. Your senses are trying to help and protect you, but any distraction or variation will break your concentration and pull you out of character.

You've already marked in your look-up moments. Now read through and mark where you need to breathe, and any dramatic pauses or changes of mood. Have you ever seen the way that musical scores have notations beyond just the notes? They have a special code to say where to breathe, or play faster, slower, louder, softer. For your purposes, pencil notes are best, right in among the words. If you habitually have a problem with building speed as you read, train yourself to slow down by putting slash marks (///) between sentences — especially sentences where you want to pause or read slowly for dramatic effect.

Use different colored adhesive notes to mark different types of reading selections — pink for romantic, blue for action, etc. This will help you choose your selections on the fly.

Character placement

Any author reading a scene in which two or more characters are taking part needs to establish character placement. This is a technique speakers can use to help the audience distinguish between voices.

If you are doing two characters, shift your shoulders and head slightly to the right for one and slightly to the left for the other. Turning only your head will look stilted; leading with your shoulder right and left, slight as the movement is, creates a whole space for each character without moving too much. The faster the exchange between voices, the smaller your movements need to be.

If you have a third character or narrator, place him/her in the middle. Practice the character transitions until they feel smooth and natural to you.

A "character spot" will help you keep things consistent for the audience. When you check out your performance area, try to find some stationary spot about eye level facing you which you can mark for each character's face. Try to pick something that won't be covered by the audience. Each time the character speaks, glance at the spot as you would glance at the speaker. No need to stare, a glance is enough to keep the character in the same place and at the same height in your spatial awareness.

Exceptions would be a character who is smaller or taller than another character. In this case you would want your spot lower or higher than eye level. But be careful! Keep the movements subtle. Your chin just ain't that interesting and neither is the top of your head. If one of your characters is a very small child, try to look up keeping your chin almost level. For very tall characters, turning your chin slightly sideways will strengthen the illusion of looking down. You'll have to lower your head a bit and that will lower your eyes. Instead, look for excuses for this tall character to look up now and then so we in the audience don't lose his face or miss the look in his eyes.

Try video taping yourself. It can be very useful to see how clearly defined your characters are. Just remember, when you watch yourself, you cannot be mesmerized by your performance — no matter how brilliant. Some film actors watch their dailies (the daily film shot before editing) and feel it is a wonderful course correct, so to speak. Other actors never look at dailies because they feel it stunts their creativity.

Whether or not you decide to tape your rehearsal, rehearsing before an audience is an absolute must. Even a tiny audience will help you make minor adjustments to your reading. More important, it will give you an idea of audience reaction. The boost this will give your self-confidence is immeasurable.

Staying focused

An interesting aspect of performing is that your brain sections itself off into categories such as the actor, the producer, the critic, the operations director. The goal is to keep the team functioning silently on your behalf while only the actor takes the stage and performs.

What if a person coughing or a baby crying or even a phone ringing threatens to spoil your performance? An actor dealing with a backdrop falling, a missing prop, another actor late for his entrance, may get the shakes. He may feel uncertain, stumble vocally, have all sorts of reactions, while his mental team huddles assessing the situation.

It is a kind of cerebral stall tactic.

But then a second calamity happens. You could call it Murphy's Law for actors: if you make one mistake, you'll make another.

You see, while you are busy reacting to the stumbled word or twisted phrase, you come right out of your suspension of disbelief. It pulls you out of the scene and is rather like being awakened when you are in the middle of a dream. It can be very disorienting.

The only way to survive is to immediately renew your focus onto the script and the scene. After a few seconds, you will be back in the groove. Your mental critic can assess the damage later. Your internal producer can analyze how this happened or what to do next time a coughing fit or crying baby happens during a performance. But the actor part of you must always lead during an actual performance.

Like an athlete, you've got to stay in the game and forget about the foul or the bad call.

After you've built your characters, practiced your readings and feel reasonably prepared, rope in an associate or two, friends or family members and give yourself a dress rehearsal. Give them all the bells and whistles.

One final note on rehearsing: unless you have a director, weigh well-meant suggestions with some care. Take all praise and divide by at least 50%. If your friend says that she gets confused as to which character was where, it's important to check your character placement. If, on the other hand, she thinks you need to wear a bustier, or a poet's shirt slit down to your waist, well, you see what we mean.

It's okay to be naked at the podium, but you can't be poorly dressed.

CHAPTER FIVE

Taking It on the Road

The true test of a Halloween costume: it's got to let you drink, dance, and fit through the Men's Room door.

Herb Tajalle

If you thought you lived with your book when you were writing it, welcome to a new phase in your relationship. Now you're getting physical. In this chapter we'll take a look at what you, as the author, have to do to take your show on the road.

Pack Mule 101

Do you have a box of your books in the trunk of your car? How much does it weigh? This is not an idle question, as you will discover the afternoon you're reading at a bookstore that's bought twelve copies of your book and the crowd is happily bigger than expected. You could sell thirty or more — if you had them. Or the day you get to a store, and despite their best efforts, they're scrambling to find any copies of your book at all. These are the moments when a box of books in the trunk of your car is valued above rubies.

But. That box of books weighs somewhere between thirty and forty-five pounds. Somebody has to pick it up and put it in the car, whether you need to take it on the plane or drive across town. And if your name isn't nationally known, and often if it is, that Somebody is you. Depending on your size and strength, you may want to break the box down into smaller packages, or invest in a folding strap-on luggage cart.

Be as self-contained as possible. What you carry with you will depend on how far you have to carry it. If you are doing a workshop or demonstration, you'll need to make a tight package of whatever you'll need. If you are using photographs or posters, the display should be sturdy, light and unbendable, such as mounted on foam core boards. And the boards should be of manageable size, so a slight breeze doesn't catch them like sails and blow you out into the traffic. Durability, cost and weight are the prime considerations.

Plan how to wrap everything up, and always think: handles. How will I carry this? Take a look at a shipping supply catalog and a luggage catalog at the same time. You'll get ideas.

Write a short introduction of yourself (printed in large type, so it's easy to read), to give to your host or presenter. They probably already have some remarks prepared, since you did send them a press kit with a background sheet when you set up the appearance. But here again, remember Murphy's Law. The one time you don't bring an intro is the one time your host will be reduced to reading your bio off the dust jacket. Besides, you want to make sure whoever introduces you has all the facts.

Make a checklist of what you'll need for your presentation:

The box of books.

A sales receipt book, in case you sell the box (or part) to the store or sponsor.

The performance copy of your book, the one with all your notes.

Any other notes, or books for your presentation.

Press kit and short introduction.

Visual aids.

Workshop handouts.

Brochures for your book and yourself.

A bottle of water and your camera.

Always rely on your checklist. Because, no matter how good your memory, if you don't have a checklist, the day will come that you will forget something.

The famous Hawaiian singer Nina Keali'iwahamana travels extensively to perform. Once she flew to Toronto to sing for the Governor General of Canada. As she was dressing to take the stage she made a horrible discovery. What she had thought was her turquoise silk pantsuit was really only her jacket — and a pair of her husband's golf pants. Five minutes to curtain. Frantic, she pinned the legs up at the ankles and made a big gather at the back of her waist, where it wouldn't show to the audience. Then she went out and sang beautifully for the Governor General. And hoped no one would figure out why she put her hand in her pants pocket every time she hit a high note.

You are what you wear

Consider your clothing as an enhancement or prop: don't ever let it overshadow you. Remember, the most important part about your reading is the audience's chance to get to know you. Keep makeup light. Keep clothing simple.

You will want to balance the kind of personal style you have with the tone and genre of your book. J. K. Rawlings of *Harry Potter* fame has done a nice job of this when making public appearances or sitting for publicity photos. She usually doesn't dress like a wizard, but she may wear a long cape or even a long sweater coat. She's worn simple, dark clothing with a long skirt and an interesting belt that gave a kind of Merlin-like feel without in any way being a costume.

If you're reading at a formal black-tie dinner about the history of clowns in American culture, we're certainly not suggesting you wear checkered pants and an oversized jacket. But you could wear an unusual pin on your tux or a rather large flower in the lapel. Not enough to scream costume, but enough to suggest an association.

No matter what, you need to be comfortable: not only comfortable as in your clothes fit well, but comfortable in how you feel about your look. Enjoy discovering ways of suggesting period and flavor, while letting your personal style shine through.

And what about hard and fast rules, you say? Yes. There are a few.

Never wear a short skirt if you plan to be sitting in a chair on a raised stage or platform. Never wear clothing that restricts movement — especially if you need to make big gestures. Reconsider a hairdo that hides your profile from the sideline audience. Be wary of long necklaces that could clink on a microphone as you lean forward.

Your mom always told you to check relevant zippers and fastenings before you make your entrance. She was right: if anything can ride up, slide down, or rip, it will most certainly do so while you are performing. Protect yourself by rehearsing in what you plan to wear. Try it out before you arrive for your reading.

Have a good Plan B you can switch to without wasting time or losing focus. If you have an outfit that was sent to the cleaners just prior to your appearance, have an alternative all worked out just in case it comes back shrunken, faded or damaged. You want to minimize any distraction of your focus, especially a negative one. With a pre-planned backup, you remain calm and confident.

In addition to making sure they're shined, here's some special advice about shoes: if they hurt, don't wear them. The ideal footwear makes you feel grounded, steady and relaxed. Uncomfortable shoes can create tension, cause headaches — yes, that's true — or trip you on your way to the podium. When they throw your balance off, they also distort your all-important mental equilibrium.

Security

If you have any security concerns, discuss them honestly with your host. It's only fair to let them know ahead of time if you are receiving bomb threats, or sinister notes from love-crazed fans. Most booksellers take the First Amendment very seriously, but they have a right to know in advance so they can get the kids off the street.

Local appearances

Begin in your own area first. Unless you live way out in the boondocks, there are at least half a dozen places you can appear within a ten-mile radius of your house. Local appearances do not make the demands on an author that touring does, and you can practice your presentation in simpler circumstances. You'll be close enough to ask a knowledgeable friend or member of your critique group to attend and give you impressions. Use these events to refine your checklist, too.

For local or regional appearances, dragoon your spouse, children, friends and relations. They should all be coming to see you anyway, right? Especially for your first few performances, pack the house with friendly faces. That way you'll feel more relaxed — and you'll have extra hands to help carry. Don't expect huge audiences unless you've got a big advertising budget, and not even then. Keep your expectations low and you'll always be pleasantly surprised.

Time yourself. Find out how long it takes you to assemble whatever program enhancements you want to use. Don't set yourself up so you have to assemble a life-sized replica of the Eiffel Tower out of matchsticks before you can begin. Keep things simple, so you stay focused on the main point of the evening.

You've already made a scouting trip, or at least called and talked with your host about the room and the situation. If you haven't had that opportunity, plan to arrive extra early so you can check the place out. Rushing in at the last moment and steaming around frantically is too stressful, and likely to lead to belly-flops. Set up quickly and with a minimum of fuss. Be professional: the staff will get a favorable impression of you, and you want to polish that impression until it shines. Don't expect the store owners to drop everything and hover around you; they've got work to do, and you are only part of it.

Debrief after every appearance. Collect comments from your host and your guests, and any observers who were helping you. If there's nobody else, ask yourself questions. Make notes about what selections you read, and what else you did for your presentation. Keep track of what worked and what didn't, and any unusual questions or reactions. This is how you make each presentation better than the one before.

Touring

A book tour can be super-intense, eighteen cities in twenty-one days, readings-interviews-media events, the kind of circus that a big publishing house puts on for your book — if they are launching it with a major push. A book tour can also be a leisurely handful of events you organize yourself around that trip to Minneapolis to visit Uncle Charlie.

When you, or the marketing person at your publishing house, begin to arrange appearances, you have to make some decisions about what you can actually do for your book. How much can you invest physically and emotionally? What effect will it have on your family and your employment?

Be realistic about what you can do. A bad back or a deathly fear of flying are certainly conditions that affect how you can tour. Likewise, if you are a brand-new mom, or happen to be in prison. Be realistic about what your publishing house can do, also. Publishers are becoming much more reluctant to hand most writers a big-ticket book tour. You know, the kind with plane tickets, hotel rooms and an escort in each city. Cheer up, this is a marketing and sales driven decision. They need to sell a lot of books to cover the cost.

If the marketing and sales decision allows for a tour, whether it's a blue plate special or one you arrange yourself, pay extra attention to your travel times and distances. You don't want to be scheduled for a presentation in Minneapolis at 3:00 and another in Milwaukee at 4:30. Or the west side of town at 10:00 and the east side at 12:15. When you call your host to ask about the venue, inquire about traffic problems as well. Their knowledge of local conditions can warn you that Interstate 34 is under construction, and that you need to allow extra time coming in from the airport. Join a motor club and use their trip planning services.

Stretch your tour budget by staying with relatives or friends wherever possible. If your publisher doesn't pay for an escort in each city, and you want help with travel from the airport to the hotel to the presentation venue, consider hiring an escort who specializes in author tours. They're available in most large cities; check the Yellow Pages under "author" or "media escorts." Contact your publisher's sales reps, too, if the house will let you. The reps are located in most major cities, but they have sales regions, so they know a lot about the stores and their communities.

Touring is harder on you, physically, than local appearances. You have to make tough decisions about what you can carry on the plane. If you've written a western, you can bring your hand-tooled silver-studded saddle to a local event, but just try and fit it into the overhead compartment on a 747. Hauling a box of books is tough enough. Plan accordingly. This is when your visual aids and other program enhancements really need to be light, compact and durable.

Take advantage of travel. For his book on coffee, Mark Pendergrast had a reading set at Eagle Harbor Books on Bainbridge Island. Riding the ferry from Seattle, he took advantage of the situation to hand out leaflets about his book to the passengers, and invited people to his reading. During the reading he sang a song he had learned when picking coffee. The event was a great success. And the next weekend someone who had met him on the ferry came into the store and bought ten copies of his book, one for each of their espresso stand operators.

Think positive, take your vitamins, and drink lots of fluids. Eat right and do what your mother told you about keeping out of drafts. Your effectiveness is cut significantly if you get sick on the trip. Not to mention your enjoyment of the process.

Exercise. You need it, it will make you feel better and you'll give a better presentation. Many hotels have exercise rooms, or arrangements with nearby health clubs. You can jog, walk, do yoga, or whatever, but exercise. Get your blood pumping every day.

You can love the nightlife all you want, but you've got to be on deck and ready to play first thing in the morning. This is business. Get your thrills from making people fall in love with your book.

Keep writing

One thing you must never lose sight of during all the excitement and activity surrounding your book appearances is — your next book. You aren't planning to stop writing now, are you? And once a publisher likes your work, they'll probably want a steady supply. If you've signed a two-book deal, they want that next one soon. Like tomorrow, or yesterday.

> PK: Many writers have to write every day to keep their creative process going. I sometimes think of the place in my brain I have

to go to write as being a room with a 500 pound door with rusty hinges. If I don't open that door for a couple of days it feels harder to open when I do get back to it. If I'm in the midst of writing a book and I don't open that door for twenty-one days, it might take me a week or more of prying to get the door open and squeeze my way back inside again. You cannot allow even a book tour to slow you down.

Make it a rule to dedicate a minimum of one hour a day to your writing. Carve it out of your schedule. You may not be able to create new copy, but you can edit previous work, expand and refine your chapter outline, work on character sketches, research or make notes for future chapters. Work on the plane, in the lobby or coffee shop, write notes on the back of your hand, if necessary. Anything that gets your head back inside the book, keeps you engaged with it, that's what you need. Keep those rusty hinges oiled, so the door will open — as easily as it ever opens — when you're home again.

Keep the home fires burning

It used to be when you went on a trip, people expected you would be out of touch while you were gone. Lack of communication was one of the charms and constraints of distance. But now with cell phones and e-mail, and business moving at such an accelerated pace, communication is too much with us.

You'll need means of checking your messages and e-mail regularly on the road. You can't afford to be cut off. Locate an Internet café, a copy center or other business facility; or maybe even a public library can help you out. It's important to have somebody to hold the fort for you, who can check your surface mail and handle your office details. Coming home to a stack of papers, half of whose deadlines have passed, is very depressing. If you can't enlist a friend, spouse or other relative, consider hiring a secretarial service. You can have your mail routed to them, if you'll be gone ten days or more, and you expect that you will have business to transact.

And call home and talk to your loved ones when you're on the road without them. This will keep you grounded in your life. You have enough to do without fighting homesickness or spousal resentment or worry over little Carol's cold. Voice to voice isn't face to face, but it keeps the home fires burning.

Taking your show on the road is part of being an author. The important thing is to be comfortable doing it. Put on your touring performer persona as if it were a good Halloween costume, one that will let you drink, dance and fit through the rest room door.

CHAPTER SIX

Stage Presence

Now I want spirits to enforce, art to enchant...
Let your indulgence set me free.

The Tempest, William Shakespeare

Stage presence. What is it, exactly?

Is it like charisma, something that you have to be born with? A blessing of the gods, like being naturally gorgeous, having perfect pitch or never gaining weight — just an unfair fluke of nature? No. Charisma may ever remain a mystery, but stage presence, what actors call "taking stage," is a skill which can be acquired. Like so much about acting, the key to stage presence lies in mental energy combined with an attitude of leadership. You have the ability within you to mentally command an audience to follow you. Of course, they want you to lead. Once the audience feels you pick up the invisible reins, they relax and you have their attention.

Again, build it and they will come. When you stand up to do a presentation, you need to start casting your spell before you even speak. And you do that by taking stage. Part of the power of taking stage is achieved by having a very clear mental focus. Most of us, at any given moment, are engaged in multi-level thinking — getting the oil changed, remembering to stop at the cleaners, pick up dog food and on and on. But when you center your focus on just one thing, your presence becomes very powerful.

If you've ever taught, or been a coach, or held a leadership position, you know what we mean. And it doesn't matter if you are shy or uncomfortable in front of people. In fact, many performers are terribly shy in person. But everyone has used this same kind of focused energy before in other situations. Think of how you centered your focus the last time you prepared to swing a golf club, or opened a letter from the IRS. Another way to describe it is gathering your mental forces. Visualize a panther crouched ready to spring, a dog waiting for a treat. Total focus.

Best of all, when you draw all your attention and energy into a single focus, any nervousness you feel can actually work for you. The adrenaline rush we get when we are nervous is part of the instinctive fight-or-flight thing.

When you are nervous, you actually think more clearly, see better, hear more sharply and have more oxygen flowing through your body. You are physically stronger in case you need to flee or fight. Whenever our bodies sense a perceived vulnerability of any kind, adrenaline surges to help ensure our survival. The fact that you feel mildly to extremely nervous only means your body understands that this performance is important to you and you are putting yourself out there, taking a risk.

So when you feel the nerves, know that it means that your body is preparing. You are at your most alert, most intelligent and most prepared. Recognize it for the extra armor it is, and not as a sign that you are in trouble. Performers can fall into the trap of seeing nerves as a sign that they are not "on their game," when actually, the exact opposite is true. Nerves will only overpower you if you take them as a sign of doom.

When you focus your energy, use your heightened senses to improve your performance. Next time you have to do something that makes you nervous, try this. When you start to feel the nerves, imagine you are climbing on top of them. Take a deep breath and think of your clearer hearing, brighter vision and increased physical strength as your secret weapons. Mount your steed and ride off to victory. Use whatever image works for you.

> MW: I am fond of visualizing Joan of Arc, but that's just me. The important thing is to see the jitters as the great help they truly are.

Okay, you may say, but what about the times I don't get nervous? In any negotiations meeting, during a hot tennis match or while performing brain surgery? Oh, yes. You do have the adrenaline. But because you are more familiar with these activities, you're likely to feel the adrenaline as a lift. And there may be less released because your mind and body are more familiar with the activity. But it is there and you use it without even realizing it. In an unfamiliar situation the adrenaline rush is obvious, maybe even a bit threatening. Just remember that it is there to help you.

Whenever you try anything for the first few times, you will feel the adrenaline more strongly. But as you get more experienced at doing readings or interviews or whatever makes you extremely nervous, the pounding waves of adrenaline will gentle and change into familiar alertness. We promise.

Now this may sound weird, but once you take stage, you can increase your stage presence very simply by mentally expanding your energy as if you were a balloon filling with air. The trick to use is mental imagery. If you need to fill a huge room, mentally expand yourself. If you are in a very small place, mentally bring your energy in close like the golden vibrating energy of the sun. Okay, it sounds really "out there." But try it. It works.

And once you take stage, realize that you and the audience will be exchanging energy. It is this marvelous exchange that actors miss most when doing film or television work. When you can feel the audience's energy coming to you, that's when you know you've got 'em! Whether an audience is hushed, laughing wildly, or just thoughtful, they are giving off energy and to accept that is to let them in. You will feel it. Use it.

Have you ever watched someone in concert and felt as though he or she didn't know you were there? It's a feeling of distance and you didn't like it, did you? That performer didn't accept and use the energy from the audience.

The main thing here is to mentally open up. Give yourself permission to be seen. A subtle thing, yes, but it can make all the difference.

When you are rehearsing in front of your support group, try it. You will begin to feel their energy and how it supports you as you work. It can also inspire you, telling you when to get bigger or smaller. You'll have to experience it for yourself. In the same way that working with another actor can fuel your creativity, the audience is truly a part of your performance. If you let them in, your performance will be better and you'll have more fun. Remember, they are partners in this enterprise.

There is a feeling inside you when you take stage. Sometimes actors describe it as becoming an instrument, a human harp that plays the author's words and feelings like music. They feel the power of the material is flowing through them. Use whatever image might work for you, you can feel the difference.

Play around with it. Stand up in your practice area and pretend that you are a king speaking to your worshipping throng, a conductor picking up his baton, a general addressing his troops, Billy Crystal at the Academy Awards. Have fun. Be victorious.

And this you must always, always remember. As Shakespeare pointed out, we are all actors. And because humans remain ever fascinated with each other, we *all* have the capacity to entertain and enchant.

> MW: Some years ago, I was asked by a university to teach two classes as an artist in residence. One class was for students in the drama department, all expecting to make performing a career. The other class was for adult students in a continuing education program.

I assumed the adult class would be more challenging and perhaps less successful.

I told my adult class that all I asked of them was to suspend their disbelief and perform for the fun of it. The analogy I used was stepping off a cliff and trusting that an invisible platform will be there. I told them that there was no right way and no wrong way, only *their* way. I called on each of them to celebrate their individual uniqueness.

In both classes we worked on the same basic skills and exercises outlined in the beginning of this book. And while I was looking forward to what my hotshot actors would do when it came time to perform their scenes and monologues, I was apprehensive for my class of inexperienced adults.

When performance day arrived, I eagerly went to my first class, the drama session. As I walked in the door I was struck by the flatness of energy. The excuses began immediately. They'd had tests, they'd been up late working on other assignments and weren't able to memorize their scripts, they had colds. Couldn't they have more time?

Of course I made them perform, but I was struck by their lack of concentration, their lack of investment. Instead of "building it" honestly, most of the students tried to paste on emotions and reactions. They were using technical tricks instead of letting the characters flow through them. I was shocked. These kids were drama students. But when I asked, they had no idea why their characters did what they did, felt what they felt, wanted what they wanted. The students had developed no backstory, no foundation for what brought their characters to their point and time in the story. They had made the classic mistake of "acting" instead of "being." For most of that group, it was just another college class they had to pass. They were only concerned about the grading, making up work and all that ya-da ya-da.

Walking over to the English building for my next class, I wondered what on earth would happen with my fish-out-of-water adults.

As I entered the classroom, I could feel the surge of energy. What a difference! And let me tell you, those shy, inexperienced performers absolutely blew my socks off!

Why? How? Not because they were brilliant and inspired. Not because they had star-power charisma like Julia Roberts or Mel Gibson. They weren't perfectly polished, but they were surprisingly poised. They each stood at the podium and "took stage." Better still, they stood, if you will, *naked at the podium*. Without lighting or makeup or costumes or sound effects or music. They were also, happily, naked in the best sense:

without artifice, allowing their personalities and experiences to shape the characters they read. Accents or devices became part of them as they suspended their disbelief. They gave themselves permission to go for it 100%. They trusted their audience to be willing and ready to like them. It was one of the most stunning and exciting moments of my life, not to mention one of the most rewarding. What a victory for each of those adults to meet their personal power and take it for a ride.

You can do it, too.

Preparation and practice are vital because your material is then familiar and comfortable. Preparation also gives you confidence that you've done everything you can to be ready for this moment, rather like getting ready for your first solo airplane flight, a piano recital or state boards. You must be prepared and you must stay in the moment.

But you can't cheat. You can't fake it. You have to surrender to yourself: step off the cliff and trust in the invisible platform.

There are no safety belts or parachutes when you stand naked at the podium.

CHAPTER SEVEN

Of Sites and Sightlines

Let's put on a show!
We can use the old barn!

Judy and Mickey

The play's the thing....

Hamlet, William Shakespeare

Most theatrical types will tell you that the set design (the physical setting where the scene takes place) is actually a key character in a play. At your presentation the site may offer very little to work with, and that's okay. But you don't want your setting to work against you.

Your goal is to create a bridge between the setting you are in and the tone and visceral feel of your book. For example, if you've written a novel of horror and psychological torture and the venue is as cheerful as a home and garden show, have your host put you in a corner with odd tropical plants or else in as neutral an area as possible. Be aware of what the surroundings say in mood and climate. If the setting is very difficult to manipulate, try at least to keep it from imposing its own mood on the reading. This is where your visual aids will help.

Earlier we discussed the importance of gathering as much information as you can about the venue where you will perform your reading. Since wonderful exposure opportunities can sometimes come in the oddest forms, keep in mind that whether you are at a bookstore or have been invited to do a reading at Sea World, your objectives will always be the same. You want to ensure that the audience:

Can see you.

Can hear you.

Is comfortable enough to relax and sail away on your words.

These are the crucial points to remember as you set up for each presentation, no matter if you're appearing at a bookstore, giving a lecture, or working the wakes, weddings and sporting events circuit.

Working with your set

Look for a way to make your setting suggest the ambiance of your book. Certainly there is a great difference between a full stage production and a reading. But there are similarities, too. One important one is that you are asking an audience to let themselves be transported. This involves their willingness and their imagination. Why not give them a helpful nudge? Using any inherent advantages your venue may have to offer helps the audience transition into the world of your subject matter. And of course, the more memorable you can make the audience's experience, the more power it will have to enhance and advance your career. Effective staging — even suggested staging — is like leather seats in a Mercedes, the candy left on your hotel pillow, candle-light for a romantic dinner. It works.

Most bookstores will have a designated reading spot, and it's not worth trying to rearrange that. The bookstore atmosphere is positive for BOOK as icon, and neutral on subject. Your visual aids will create the set and the staging for your book.

If a setting turns out to have problems, you have to make the best of it, though it's perfectly fine to make reference to the fact. If there are posts in front of a couple of segments of the audience, commiserate with those people who won't see the performance well. Sometimes a gentle joke — "I see the late-comers have been stuck behind the shame-on-you posts again," or "We still have seats in the peek-a-boo view section" — can break the ice and also let the audience know that you are aware of their problem and wish you could do more for them. If you have sightline problems, move around a bit during your presentation to make sure you can see every face at least part of the time. If that's not possible, and you have a Q & A period after-wards, do walk around a bit for that.

But what about a presentation where you don't have a pre-set location? For some people, that's as scary as facing a blank sheet of paper. How do you decide what to do? Here are some examples of thinking out-side the square.

Country club

So let's say you've been invited to do an appearance and reading for a group that meets at a posh country club. If you've written a steamy, South American story of doomed love you'd want to read by the swimming pool, weather permitting. If possible, have the appearance in the late afternoon or a warm evening with lots of soft lighting, stronger lighting on you, of course.

How about a brooding murder mystery? Try the library or even the lobby of the clubhouse, if it has enough dark furniture in it and an over-stuffed ambiance. For humorous material, go for a lighter, more airy-feeling room. If you've written a cookbook, what about a dining area of some kind, which could accommodate your audience. It would be great fun to hear a cookbook author in a large, open kitchen, wouldn't it? That may be unlikely, but what you are working toward is using your setting to help get the audience in the mood. Think about how an unusual venue might make the presentation more enjoyable and memorable.

Wouldn't it have been a treat to hear Emily Dickinson read her poetry on a sun-dappled afternoon, sitting on a blanket under a tree? Or Roald Dahl reading in the children's playroom of a mansion? A travel book about Africa would be fun to listen to at the zoo. For science fiction or something otherworldly, you might be better off with a minimal setting. Be in a room with all the lights off except for a light on you, for example. Let the scenery come from your words and the listeners' imaginations. Think of the sets that might be used in a movie version of your book and see how the venue you will be in might work to create the suggestion of scene. Is there a grand old ballroom, or a room with oak paneling?

Outdoor venues

Presenting outdoors offers terrific opportunities to enhance your book. A mountain-climbing book will profit by a view of mountains, a garden book from being presented in a garden. What about a book of love poetry, backlit by a sunset in June? You can't buy a more effective set. But it's well to remember that presenting outdoors leaves you at the mercy of wind and weather.

Weather

Weather rules are reminiscent of baseball. If it rains, you don't play; but you should dress and wait in the dugout, in case it lifts enough to squeeze in your innings. Keep a tarp over everything until you're ready to play — dry cleaner's bags are good. As days get colder and later in the year, the crowds are smaller — unless you're going to the playoffs. Dress for the field conditions. Bring layers, if you're doubtful, and ask if your host has a backup plan.

Wind

Dealing with the wind is another matter. Just as it can carry a baseball or hold it back, the wind can carry or hold back your voice. Outdoor venues, if they are bigger than a backyard patio, should be miked. Voice placement (see Chapter One) is really important now, to give the mike the clearest, best-projected sound. Emphasize placement in your warm-up. If the wind is blowing from your back toward the audience, visualize your voice riding it like a wave. If it blows in your face, go lower in your vocal register, and aim your voice under the wind, not into it. Don't try to out-scream it, you'll only hurt your throat. Pull all the people in tight, this is a good excuse. Open your throat as though yawning (see the dropped-jaw photo in Chapter Eight) and direct your voice to the back row of listeners.

Most important: ask if everybody can hear. Establish what your speaking levels need to be right at the beginning. It won't make you sound like an amateur, it will demonstrate your commitment to your audience. Pay attention to the faces in the back, if they get restless, you may not be reaching them.

If the wind is cold, and liable to be uncomfortable, consider pieces you might skip to cut your presentation short. However, unless people are in absolute distress, you should not skimp what they came for. Watch the body language of the people on the edges of the crowd. They'll be your best guide to how the rest are feeling.

Consider your visual aids. Big, flat, lightweight displays are going to fly away. Can they be laid flat, and perhaps just held up for their moment of attention? If there's anything flapping, like a sign, or the skirt of a table, this is a distraction for the audience, and for you. Try to tie it down or remove it, or ask a friend to lean on it. Don't fight a distraction. Fix it.

The wind likes papers and notes, the looser the better. And to fling your scarf in your face, or blow your hat away. Think about everything you plan on wearing and carrying on a windy day. What do you have in your pockets that you could use as a paperweight? Be flexible, and hold onto your sense of humor. Anger and frustration mess up your concentration. Shut them out and focus on your presentation.

> PK: Once I had a speaking engagement at the California Shakespeare Festival. They have a lovely outdoor theatre in the Berkeley Hills. I'd seen pictures of it on the CSF Web site. There were pictures, too, of the grove of eucalyptus trees where I would speak. They had a nice wooden podium, leveled, with a handsome lectern on it, and a microphone. That afternoon was hot and sunny, so the shade was nice. Though the audience sat scattered at picnic tables and on logs, the sound system let me reach everybody just fine. But the wind! It was warm enough, not uncomfortable, but blowing hard enough to turn your umbrella inside out.
>
> The presentation began well, and I added some historical California Shakespeare stories for local interest. I was sailing along. And then the wind grabbed my notes and blew them away. I reached frantically for the two sheets, snatched them in mid-air, fell off the podium, rolled over twice and came to

my feet with the papers crumpled in my fists. Breathing heavily, I remounted the podium, laid out my notes on the lectern, and smoothed them down. Then I looked up at the audience and said, "I'll have you know I planned that."

When they stopped laughing, I delivered the rest of my presentation to an audience of friends.

Sun

If you are to be placed in direct sun, watch out for glare. Avoid the necessity of sunglasses; you want eye contact. You want to see, and you want to be seen. Protect yourself against sunburn, that sizzling feeling really cuts into your concentration. If you wear a hat, show some forehead — again, so they can see your eyes. Choose a style that doesn't block your profile.

Heat and sun exposure may fade or melt some of your props. Photographs and fabrics are especially vulnerable. If the items are built just for the tour, set them out there unless they'll melt. But if they're items of value, some shade should be contrived, or you are justified in showing them only briefly at the appropriate moment in the presentation.

Noise

Background noise is an issue outdoors, and a major reason for using a mike. Our urban/suburban culture assaults us with fire trucks, chain saws, heavy construction, loud music. Any site within a twenty-mile radius of a major airport has those days when the wind is just in the right direction, and the jets seem to be coming right overhead every three minutes.

If the problem is a steady noise, you may be able to overcome it by expanding your voice (see Chapter One) or asking your host to turn up the volume. A fire truck is usually a one-time event — unless you're next door to the station — something you can make a brief comment on and then continue. The jet problem is harder to combat. About the best you can do is circle the wagons, get everybody to move down close, take it in stride, make a joke about it, and turn it into a shared experience. Time your best lines for the quiet moments in between.

Indoor or outdoor, upstairs or down, the key thing to remember is this: the stage setting for your presentation can be a key character in your performance, but your book is the star.

Do what you can to make the setting work and then forget about it. If you are really into your presentation you can make it a memorable experience for your audience. No matter what.

After all, as Shakespeare said, "The play's the thing...."

CHAPTER EIGHT

Warming Up

Act enthusiastic and you'll __be__ enthusiastic!

Dale Carnegie

Today is Presentation Day. You're appearing at a bookstore or a library, or maybe you're at the garden show with your new mystery *Death and Peatmoss.* You've got a one-hour time slot.

You have to be a two-headed monster today: one is the performer, the other is the business person. The performer has to warm up the instrument, and play the music. The business person has to take care of the details.

Right now, let's warm up the instrument. These pre-show practices and techniques are long-honored tricks performers have used for years to make sure they have every advantage physically and mentally.

Care and feeding

Be aware of what you are eating and drinking prior to any kind of public speaking. At the start of the day, plan to get enough water. Pour yourself a large glass first thing in the morning and drink it all because being well hydrated lubricates the voice and helps muscles stay loose and flexible. Time of day can make a big difference, too. Let's flesh out the various scenarios.

Say you are appearing at a mall at ten in the morning. Even if you never eat breakfast, make sure you have something in your stomach. Growling stomachs are not attractive and a lack of protein is sure to give you the jitters or the shakes — especially when you are tense or a bit nervous. If you are not a big breakfast eater, a hard-boiled egg will do the trick. Or a bagel with jam, instead of cream cheese. Toast and peanut butter is okay, the stickiness dissolves rapidly and the protein is very good.

Whatever you choose, make sure you get plenty of protein and go lighter on the carbohydrates, which actually make most people hungrier faster. If you're delayed in starting your performance, you don't want to get light-headed.

Always stay away from dairy products for at least three hours before performing. Milk products coat the throat and make you feel and sound "thick." Dairy is also slower to digest than other forms of protein, which may cause problems. Even if you can't stand your morning coffee without milk, skip it if you have less than three hours before you do your presentation.

If you do drink coffee at the venue, follow it with a glass of water to lubricate the throat. Coffee can sometimes make the mouth membranes dry and can be a culprit in lips-sticking-to-the-teeth syndrome. And of course, too much coffee or tea can cause caffeine jitters. If you're feeling very dry-mouthed from nerves, or if your throat is scratchy from a cold, hard candy is a very good lubricant. Many performers have some kind of lozenge ready to pop into their mouths moments before going on.

For afternoon or evening performances, the same rules apply. Make sure you've eaten, ideally at least two hours before your appearance. Concentrate on light proteins and a salad. If you are scheduled to speak after a meal, eat lightly and drink plenty of water. Obviously, avoid problem foods like beans, and any food that makes you burp. Soda pop should be avoided for the same reason, and it does nothing to re-hydrate you.

It's probably best to skip all alcohol because it dehydrates you and takes away your edge. A small amount of white wine is okay if you are not performing for at least an hour after drinking it, but in general water is always your best beverage bet.

Warm-up routines

Whatever time of day you are scheduled for, try to give yourself time alone to warm up. Just as any athlete warms up before a game or meet, you need to do your breathing and a few vocal exercises before your presentation.

Breathing: do *The Straw*— lying down, if possible — and make sure to do two counting breaths where you breathe in through the straw, then exhale, counting out loud until all the air is gone. Remember to feel as though only the numbers are coming out. Or if this image works better for you, concentrate on the numbers riding out on a wave of air.

Vocal Exercise —
DROPPED JAW

Sing or say *me may ma mo moo*
several times at higher and lower pitches,
to warm up the whole vocal range,
keeping your jaw loose.

Vocal Exercise —
RED LEATHER, YELLOW LEATHER

This is one of the most effective ways
to relax the jaw and get the tongue flexible.

Stare at a single spot on the floor or the wall.
Repeat this phrase:

> *Red Leather, Yellow Leather*
> *Red Leather, Yellow Leather*
> *Black Leather, Yellow Leather*
> *Black Leather, Yellow Leather*

Keep repeating this over and over, gradually
gaining speed. Most people find this very
challenging. The trick is to start slowly enough
so that you can say the whole thing through
once without tripping. Then gradually pick up
the pace. The first few times you can read
the lines, if you like. The more focused your
concentration is, the better you'll
do. The tongue twister serves
two functions. It centers you,
and it loosens up your tongue.
Don't let your jaw tighten, this
will only make things worse.

If your day is a frantic one,
you can do "Red Leather,
Yellow Leather" in the car,
driving to your event.

Also do a few *Mama Dolls.* (See Chapter One to review *The Straw* and *Mama Doll.*)

Not only will these exercises loosen you up and help prevent fumbled words when you perform, this is a great time for your mind to let go of other concerns and get focused on your performance. If you have time, a run-through of your presentation is a great idea. But if you only have ten or fifteen minutes, do your *Straw* breathing, the *Mama Doll* exercise and recite a few tongue twisters.

The last minute

Whether or not you've had the opportunity to have a warm-up time and/or a rehearsal prior to arriving at your event site, it never hurts to find an out-of-the-way corner once you're there. Do a modified version of *The Straw* sitting down or standing against a wall, and a little *Red Leather, Yellow Leather.* Performers often visit the restroom a few minutes prior to beginning their performance and stretch a bit and quietly vocalize in that private space.

If you find yourself feeling tense, you can even do some stretches and take some nice full breaths while sitting at your seat in a hall or at a banquet table. Concentrate on filling up your rib cage and then exhaling slowly, of course looking quite nonchalant all the while. This will calm you down and help focus your energy.

Remember, your audience wants to like you. They want to have a good time. You have something to give them. When you stand up to read, your job is to give your audience a gift. One you believe in. Concentrate on sharing your material and you'll be off to a great start.

Recovery

Now we know this is not a perfect world. So what about the huge traffic tie-up that makes you late? The cancelled flight, the unavoidable delay? You're late: you haven't had time to warm up. You're feeling completely flustered and frustrated. You can tell you are not in the performance zone. They are introducing you. The audience has been waiting and is not all that thrilled, right at the moment. What do you do?

Ignore your visual aids, for the moment, or let someone else deal with them. Grab your notes, reading copy, and whatever else you need. Take a deep breath and gather yourself before you speak. Audiences are surprisingly forgiving. Use this opportunity to connect with them — everybody has had "the day from hell." Start by letting them know how glad you are to finally be there. Apologize for making them wait. Don't grovel, but let them know your concern about being late, and your helplessness to arrive sooner. While you are having this little chat with your audience, two things are happening. You relax and buy time to get focused, and the audience has a chance to refocus as well. You can even breathe deeply and sigh if you want to.

Joking a bit with the audience about what has happened to you makes you real. It also helps everyone move past the delay. You want the audience members to buy your book. You want them to enjoy hearing you read. A quick quip about getting lost or sitting in gridlock is all you want. Don't whine. The audience can empathize, sympathize and share in your experience. Now they are rooting for you and feel that they know you. With a smile and a full breath, you begin your presentation.

MW: Some years ago I was driving to an important audition in Los Angeles, beautifully made-up, on top of the world, when something flew in the open window of the car and smacked me right in my left eye. My eye instantly clenched itself tight as a fist and began sending SOS messages of screaming pain. Seems boulders and contact lenses make poor roommates. Tears gushed down my cheek. Half-blinded, I swerved to the left shoulder of the road and stalled the car, frantic to get my contact lens out now, Now, NOW!

When at last I got the lens out and rinsed the eye and the little pain needles stopped stabbing me, I took a look at myself in the rear-view mirror. The right side of my face was still beautifully made-up. The left side appeared to have been through a car wash; I had mascara all the way down to my collar. The mirror also revealed a police car pulling up behind me. Oh, great, he's going to give me a huge ticket. To cap everything, though, I realized I hadn't brought my makeup with me, and I'd end up late, walking into the audition just the way I was. (Make a note, ladies: always carry makeup for emergencies!)

Life has some funny ways of teaching us to stay open and have faith in the outcome. The policeman's first words were, "Miss, are you all right?" He was worried about me! When I was together again, he used his lights to make way for me to get back onto the freeway and on my way. At the casting office I held my head high and, with what I hoped was a slightly ironic smile announced myself to the receptionist. When I did my audition, I had a fabulous time with the casting people. I made them laugh with my incredible story. I joked about wanting them to see how changeable my appearance could be. It turned out to be one of the most fun, friendly and relaxed auditions I'd ever done. And, oh yes — I got the part.

We have a choice in how we react to events. Do we panic? Or do we look for ways to make things work? There is almost always an advantage or an opportunity hiding in every mishap. Dale Carnegie, one of the first teachers of effective public speaking, was fond of saying, "Act enthusiastic and you'll be enthusiastic!" It sounds really trite. But it works. So does acting like you're confident.

Those few seconds before you begin your presentation are rather like standing on a diving board. You've climbed up there. You have to commit yourself as you step off to walk into the dive. Mentally you gather your focus. Physically you let go and allow the muscles to do what they know how to do. You visualize the dive. You let go. You take your three steps and let yourself pounce on the board. Your arms, legs, chest and head all work together. You become the dive.

In the same way, you gather yourself together at the podium. You feel yourself begin the character or the scene, and off you go.

A great teacher once said the secret of a happy life was to do just three things: show up, do something, and have fun. These same three rules apply to performing. This is the ultimate advice. Show up. Do what you have practiced, but feel free to make adjustments as necessary and as the Muse of live performances moves you to do. And have fun!

CHAPTER NINE

Engaging Your Audience

What did you think of the audience?
Loved her, can't stand him!

Hans Conreid

Expect the unexpected is certainly good advice when approaching any kind of live audience performance. Unfortunately, there are no special rules, no magic bullets and no escape hatches. As David Letterman is fond of saying, "What's a mother to do?" Perhaps the best piece of advice when dealing with live audiences is to remember that you want to build a bridge between yourself and your audience.

Part of the vicarious thrill of a good story is the safety of connecting to experiences through someone else. Even when we are being fascinated by a character that seems totally unlike us — Hannibal Lector, for example — isn't it the way in which we can and do relate to him that makes him so horrifying? When the Hunchback of Notre Dame stares at the camera, confused eyes peering out of his pathetic and yet hideous face, it is our own heartbreak that we recognize. Through him we reconnect with the times in our lives when our naïveté and vulnerability have been misused. We know exactly how he feels. Watching Julia Child we may relate to her messiness. We can revel in the thought that we might be as creative as she is, since we're not fussy about measuring food either.

First impressions

The first impression your audience will get of you is with their eyes. To help you build that bridge to the audience, as you approach the podium you want your body language and your mental energy to be saying, "I'm just like you, except that I've scaled Everest and I'm going to tell you about it." Or, "I'm like you are except for the fact that my horror story ideas have made me millions and I'm going to do a reading from one of them today."

Research with animals has shown what appears to be their ability to "read" a human's mind pictures. When a person pictured patting and comforting a frightened cat stuck in a tree, the cat calmed down enough to be helped out of the tree, and the rescuer did not get scratched. Who's to say that mental images don't work for people, too? While we're not suggesting that you picture yourself scratching the audience's ears, we do recommend mentally seeing the audience as warmly receiving you as you walk toward the podium, get settled and look out with a smile to welcome them.

Once you've been introduced you might like to say a few words about yourself or how you came to be a writer. Biographies are so popular because we love learning about another person's formative experiences. It's fun and fascinating to discover elements we never would have guessed.

Childhood polio forced Alan Alda to spend hours alone in his room reading. The stories he read in those books caused his lifelong fascination with people and why they do what they do. This ultimately led him to a successful career as an actor. Bet you didn't know that, did you? In just those three sentences, you've learned something very personal about Alan Alda that has given you a deeper insight into his makeup. You know him better and feel more connected to his life.

Janis Joplin was so hurt by cruel remarks about her looks in high school that, when she returned to her home town as a star, she was visibly shaken and nearly cried when a local interviewer asked her how it felt to return. Despite her hard and garish appearance, the woman underneath was a sweet, shy little girl who desperately wanted to feel pretty and be accepted. The freak show was her armor and it didn't do the job. That pain showed in her music. When you know the source, it gives her music so much more resonance.

The way you frame or introduce your reading is very important. Find your own amusing, tender, or ironic anecdote and share it with the audience. "This is the story of my daughter's descent into depression which led to her suicide. I wrote this book in the hopes that no other parent will have to go through what I have. In this part of the book, I had just found her diary and stood in her room wondering if I dared open it." Wow! We're empathetic, connected and ready to go.

Or, "When I was a little girl, my Italian grandmother lived with us. She would lay out sheets of her fresh pasta dough over the clothesline in our backyard. To me, they were angel's clouds and cooking has been magical ever since. I'm going to teach you how to use Nana's secret ingredients to make Neapolitan pasta with Zambini sauce. The best in the world!" Again, a solid connection has been made and the audience is ready to go. It's a good idea to create a couple of introductions you feel good about and then run them by your critique group, friends and family.

Okay. Your energy is focused, warm, open and accepting. You begin. How is the audience reacting to you? Usually you can get a sense fairly quickly if the audience is engaged and relaxed. Your short introduction has given them time to get used to your appearance, the sound of your voice and the kind of energy you have. The audience members, of course, are not really aware of this process. But it is an important subconscious adjustment to visual and vocal stimuli.

All that is well and good, you say. But do you do your risqué comedy reading when you look out and the "mature audiences only" crowd has brought their children? What about hecklers? What about background noise?

Noise

As we discussed in Chapter Seven, noise can be a real issue with book readings outdoors. Now let us consider it indoors. Even if the piped music is turned off, in a large store you will still have intercom paging and, of course, phones ringing. As we've said before, always opt for the quietest corner in the store. If you are familiar with a particular bookstore and you know there will be background noise, make sure you choose a more rambunctious section of your book as your reading selection.

For example, when you are reading poetry and your selection is quiet and insightful, you may have to just push through it. If you are in the middle of a stanza and the intercom goes off, just pause, smile and back up just a bit. A line or two, or the beginning of the stanza is enough, so that the audience can get back into it. The second or third time there is a major interruption you might want to pause and after three or four seconds, go on or start with that one line again.

If you're reading something light and humorous you can make a joke about it or pause and say something like, "before we were interrupted, Hubert had just discovered his pants were unzipped…" and then go on with your reading. In most cases, the audience looks to you, the performer, for a reaction. If you refuse to be thrown, they usually hold it together, too.

Never allow your concentration to go; then you will lose them for sure. There is no right or wrong way to handle distractions and noise of this kind except to apologize for it. You can say, "Shame about the noise, but we'll just tune it out together," or something like that. Audiences want the performer to be in control. By saying, "sorry, sorry, sorry," you give the impression of having no control. It is a message to the audience that you are bothered or incapacitated by it. Then you really are sunk. Just remember, you are not the cause of the distraction. If you hold focus, so will the audience.

For noise that is irritating but not impossible, joke briefly about it and then grab the reins and ride on. Or simply pause, as though of course you have this noise at a bookstore or in a mall. See if you can use the pauses you make due to the intercom or phones appear as though they were for dramatic effect.

If the noise is impossible, stop. Let the audience know you realize this isn't working. Then do what you can to move or get the noise reduced before continuing.

> PK: I was reading a love poem at my son's wedding in Honolulu when suddenly all hell broke loose in the street outside the church. Unbeknown to us, an elephant from a circus at the nearby Blaisdell Center had killed its trainer and battered its way out of the building. Now it was rampaging down Beretania Street toward a crowd of people. At the last moment, the beast was brought down in a hail of gunfire by members of the Honolulu Police Department.
>
> Inside the church, we knew none of this. All we knew was the noise — sirens, screams, elephant trumpeting, gunshots! Of course I stopped. What else could I do? The whole congregation was as distracted as I was.
>
> When the gunshot echoes had faded, the distant screams had dwindled down and the last sirens turned off, I took a deep breath and centered myself. We were there for a purpose. I had to finish.

I decided that I couldn't just pick up from where I'd left off. Gathering the people with a look, I said, "May I begin again?" Then I said the words I wanted to say, the way I wanted to say them, to an audience who was prepared to listen.

The kids had a beautiful wedding, but the video picked up some unusual sound effects.

Hecklers

A distraction coming from the audience presents a different challenge. In the most common venues for book readings you certainly wouldn't expect the audience to include drunks or hecklers, but with a live performance anything is possible. There are no foolproof tricks for handling an obnoxious or inconsiderate audience member. That's the bad news. The good news is that if you trust your instincts, you'll probably come up with a solution that works reasonably well. Stay in control. If possible, try to be amused at the person's pathetic attempts to steal the spotlight. Or be gently sympathetic for the person with what seems like a life-threatening coughing jag.

Frequently a heckler will quiet down if you ask him if he would like to read from his book or if she has an act, perhaps she could have the stage after you. It doesn't always work, but in most cases when you ask them they either shut up or at that point get worse. Never get in a shouting match. It's perfectly acceptable to ask the manager or your host to escort someone out who is impossible to deal with. The audience usually bands together when things like this happen, and will be even more supportive of you if you keep a gentle hand on the reins.

A public library audience, since library events are open to the general public, may contain people who would not normally attend your presentation. When Jim Lehrer was touring with his novel, *Purple Dots,* he spoke at the downtown public library in Seattle. Toward the end of his Q & A period, a hand went up at the back of the room, and a gentleman rose to his feet. "Why are you writing about this?" he demanded. "Why aren't you writing about the one man who matters to us all, Jesus Christ, our Lord and Savior?" Mr. Lehrer replied courteously, "But sir, that book has already been written."

Selections

In Chapter Two, we discussed having several different selections to read from any time you are booked. That way, if you expect a quiet atmosphere and it turns out to be noisy, you can use a less introspective reading. If you are expecting a large crowd and end up with just a few listeners, you may want to choose a more sensitive passage. And if your book contains some racy scenes and you find the audience unexpectedly full of children, select scenes that are a little more toned down. Planning for the unexpected keeps your options open and helps you be ready to succeed no matter what the challenge may be.

And it's not a bad idea to have some material ready for an encore. Make sure the selection you bring is at least as interesting/fun/colorful/tender as the reading you've just done. Encores are the frosting on the cake, so make sure yours is sweet.

Taking stage

As you are performing, make sure to maintain eye contact with your audience. If the group is very large, look at listeners in a section-by-section manner. If the group is very small and physically close to you, or you find making eye contact upsetting or distracting, try looking at people's eyebrows or foreheads, as we discussed in Chapter Four.

Always use an audience's energy when you can, but if eye contact won't work this technique will keep you from looking down at the floor or up at the ceiling — a real kiss of death. Keep trying to make eye contact as you develop your performance, though. It is absolutely the most powerful way to perform.

Stand with your weight on both feet. Many readers, especially at a podium, have a tendency to sway or continually shift their weight from foot to foot. It is impossibly distracting to an audience and makes you look unfocused yourself. Keep your energy centered in your diaphragm area and send it out to the audience.

Be careful to keep your movements meaningful. Gestures should come out of the story or the subject and not out of extra energy that is not being focused. If you've got the habit of scratching your head or using your hands too much, videotape yourself practicing and see how you are doing at eliminating those personal mannerisms. Or you can have someone in your support group sit in on a practice, and stop you every time you slip and do the gesture.

If you are just getting started as a public speaker/reader, the tendency may be to speak too rapidly, running sentences together. This makes listener comprehension difficult and could cause you to run out of breath — making you even more nervous and more prone to go even faster. If you feel yourself speaking a little too quickly, make each breath you take bigger. Make an effort to actually pause for the breath and imagine you have a huge halo of golden energy waves around you.

Most writers have a wonderful sense of the rhythm of their writing and they use their voices to add color and spice to the work. Relaxing into your breathing will help keep you from the race-walk style of reading that can befall anyone hit with a bit more nerves than they expected to have.

Q & A success

The question-and-answer period is the final portion of your presentation, and comes right before the book sales begin. So don't assume an overly relaxed posture which seems to say, "Whew, glad that's over. Can't wait to get outta here." Don't cling to the furniture or cross your arms tightly. That makes you look nervous and/or defensive. Instead, convey an air of openness and availability to questioners.

Have plenty of information on your topic, especially if you've written a nonfiction book. Knowing other authors who write on your subject and being able to describe the differences between the recipes you'll find in their cookbooks versus yours is informative and fun for the audience.

Anticipate the kinds of questions you might reasonably expect. Make a list and jot down answers for them before your appearance. This reduces the risk of drawing a blank. It's fine to have your list with you on stage.

Before taking the first question, thank your listeners for being a great audience. Realize that some people may wish to leave at this point. Don't show irritation if they have to excuse themselves before you begin serving dessert. Take that first question, and repeat it loudly enough to cover any chair noise from those departing.

If there are no questions immediately, stay calm. Don't wait until the silence gets embarrassing. Here's where your planning ahead pays dividends. Use some of the questions from your anticipation list as samples you can throw out, and then answer yourself. If you've tried three or four questions and no one responds, or looks likely to do so, then thank your audience and end the Q & A.

Repeat or paraphrase each question. This enables everyone to hear the question and participate in the sharing of information, and gives you more time to organize your reply.

If you don't know, *say so*. Nothing makes you look worse than trying to fake something. We take that back. One thing is worse: yawning as someone asks a question. The question may seem unimportant to you, but it is probably important to the person who asked it.

Look at the entire audience while responding to a question. This keeps them engaged in what's going on. Chances are the question you are answering is one some-one else in the audience would like to have asked. When you include all of the audience, they can feel as though you are still talking to them.

Even if asked one you think you've already covered, answer all questions gracefully. Perhaps the listener temporarily tuned out, or you were unclear. You may find an additional insight to share on the subject that you missed mentioning before.

Be brief and concise. This gives more people the opportunity to ask their questions and allows you to finish before you are exhausted. Long-winded answers can lose an audience pretty quickly. And an over-long Q & A session can turn them off, too. You don't want their last impression to be, "That was great, but I thought it would never end!" Cut it off before it begins to drag. Leave them wanting more, is always good advice.

Stalking the unpredictable audience

When actors do a long-running play, there is a tremendous temptation to copy what worked in past performances. An actor will arch a brow on a certain line and get a big laugh. Naturally, being the gluttons for praise that all performers are, we want that big laugh the next night. But the surest way to kill it is to try to do exactly the same thing, exactly the same way. Why?

Because then it isn't fresh and new — which is what drew the laugh in the first place. It has become a canned move. The only way to duplicate the laugh is to create anew the same feelings that led to the arched brow.

And even then, don't count on it. Your performance is a living thing, and will never be the same two nights running. Every show is a new show.

Finally, remember that audiences are living, breathing entities, too, and you won't always read them correctly. Small audiences can fool you. They tend to be quieter and you may think they are bored or not enjoying your presentation. That could be, but sometimes, they are just quiet and totally engrossed in what you are doing. Some audiences are comfortable laughing loudly; other groups simply smile, but are equally amused. If you typically get a big laugh in one section of your reading and you don't get it, don't be alarmed. The worst thing you can do as a performer is to let your mental director in. The minute your head goes out of the material you have lost your power and chances are good that you'll make a mistake.

Whenever you are rattled by an unusual reaction, dig in harder. Focus more energy on the material. But don't force things. Don't overdo. Stay true in your own sense of the piece. You may feel flat during the performance only to be told by those in the audience that they've never seen anything so brilliant. And you'll have times when you think you are so hot you surely will catch fire and then discover the audience has been lukewarm to the entire show. Go figure. Honor each reading and give it your best.

MW: The truth is, you are not always the best judge of how a performance is going. I had the great good fortune of doing Mary Manning's adaptation of James Joyce's "Finnegan's Wake." The play ends with a monologue several pages long. Ana Livia, the female lead, talks about the ebb and flow of her life as she prepares to die. It is a breath-taking piece, a woman's life journey but written in Joyce-speak with words that are really unintelligible. The first performance, I was worried about how the audience would respond. They seemed very quiet but I stayed the course. After the play, a woman from the audience approached me with tears streaming down her face. She grabbed my hand and said, "I didn't understand a single word you said, but I know how you feel!" You never know.

Another time I had the delicious fun of working with the late Hans Conreid. One night we had a very small, quiet audience and he came off stage and said, "It's so quiet, I can hear the lights changing." But when the play ended, that oh-so-quiet audience gave us thunderous applause. Another evening, the house was packed but it was so quiet we wondered if they were alive. Hans came back stage. He looked at me with the most mischievous smile and said, "What do you think of the audience? Loved her, can't stand him!"

CHAPTER TEN

On-site Etiquette

To succeed in the world,
we do everything we can to appear successful.
Françoise, Duc de la Rochefoucauld

To be a successful author you have to appear as one; that is, act in the ways that make an author successful. This is not acting like a "star," which is unattractive. It is acting in ways that promote your book and your career.

Your goal is to leave your hosts with the desire to invite you back again. You want them to be repeat customers, ready and waiting for your next book.

Here are some tips to promote yourself, your book and your career:

Arrive early.

Introduce yourself to the staff and meet with your host.

Ask permission to take a host/staff picture.

Meet fellow authors, if any.

Set up appropriately.

Be prepared for autographing.

Make a graceful exit.

Follow-up afterwards.

Arrive early

Nothing produces more stomach acid for a bookseller than to watch the minutes trickle past, looking at the audience they've managed to coax into attending, wondering if the author is going to show up. Think of these presentations as job interviews for your book. Would you show up late for a job interview? The message you send is that you have more important things to do, and you just managed to fit the interview in. If you are on the short list for the Nobel Prize in Literature, maybe you can afford to take that approach. Otherwise, arrive early.

Introduce yourself to the staff and meet with your host

As soon as you arrive, check in with your host. At a bookstore, ask the cashier for the contact person you've been corresponding with. That way they know you're there, and can cross off an item on their mental list of worries. Be positive and organized. Your show starts the minute you walk in the door — the show you're presenting for the staff.

Collect the names of all the people who work at the store, or for the organization. If you have the usual memory like a leaky balloon, write the names down on a business card or notepad. Pay particular attention to any salespeople. These are the people who will hand-sell your book for days and weeks and months after you have come and gone. These people are vital to your book's chances of survival.

> PK: I asked bookstore owners, "If you could tell authors one thing before they came into your store, what would it be?" I was struck that Christy McDanold of Secret Garden Bookstore in Seattle, and Gail Paul, the Community Service Manager of a Barnes & Noble Booksellers, responded in identical words. They said, "That we're on your side. That we're trying our best for you."

Your first concern is books — a last check, do they have enough? There is a box of books in your trunk, isn't there? If you've requested any special equipment necessary for your presentation — slide projector, easel and pad, whatever — now is the time to find out if all the pieces are there and everything works. Or what you may have to improvise. Deal with what is, not what was promised. Don't blow your focus or make anyone feel guilty. Stay positive. Swear if you must, but do it after the show.

And if you have any last minute security concerns, be sure to discuss them with your host. Are there pickets outside? Is your archenemy in the audience? Share that information, so the staff can help you.

Ask permission to take a host/staff picture

A good trick is to bring your camera and have a photograph taken of yourself with the staff, or at least those members most connected with your visit. This may be harder than herding cats, so don't push it, but it's a nice thing to have for your followup. And get the names right, so you can caption the photograph later. If you want to use it in a newsletter or on your Web site, you need to get written permission. Do it now.

Meet your fellow authors, if any

If you're part of a group appearance, or you're one of a series of authors appearing, do some homework. Brush up on your fellow authors; learn a little about their work. This is a great chance to network. Preparation on your part can pay dividends, and it's good manners, besides. You are, after all, members of the same tribe.

Even if your books are in widely diverse fields, the business of writing remains the same. They may know the name of a great copyright lawyer, or of a health care plan for writers. If your books are at all in related fields, they may know a good editor, or agent. Learn who they are ahead of time; they'll be flattered, and they'll think of you kindly. Maybe you can get a blurb from them for your next book. Who knows? Be prepared.

Set up appropriately

Now you set your scene. Make a final assessment of the space where you will be presenting. Where and how will you display your visual aids? Is there enough room for your demonstration?

Most bookstores are pros at this, but if you are appearing at a store and the management really hasn't thought about where they will put you, suggest a corner as far away from the main entrance as possible. You don't want the audience distracted by people milling past who are not paying attention to what you are doing. Certainly if you are making an appearance and say, doing a book signing without a reading, then you'll want to be at the front of the store to draw people in. But if you are doing a reading and then signing your book, suggest that the reading take place in the quietest section of the store. Then move to a pre-set table toward the front for the signing.

Make sure you will have adequate light, with no glare in your eyes when you look out into the audience. When you do your pre-performance visit, also note the ventilation and heating; or if you can't visit, be sure to ask if the room tends to be chilly or warm. You know how they say animals can smell fear? Audiences can, too. And they pick up on the performer's comfort level. They want to relax and not worry about anything. If you seem uncomfortable or worried, they will wonder why. An audience can't be completely invested in a presentation when they sense something is wrong.

This is the moment when all your designing, all your preparation will pay off. You want to set up swiftly, with minimum frustration. Do try to refrain from turning your back to the gathering audience and bending over. Few of us look our best from that angle. Tuck your packing materials neatly out of the line of sight. Keep the image you present clean and focused. Try to complete everything while leaving yourself some personal focus time before Zero Hour.

Your host may wish to delay the start time to give latecomers a chance to find seats, but don't count on it. You should be ready to burst out of the box anyway, remember? The first two minutes are really crucial. You want to hit the ground running.

Microphones

Make sure there has been a sound check before you go on. Sometimes this can be accomplished by the person introducing you. But for more formal settings, inquire if a technician has done the sound check. You'd think that would be obvious, but trust us, and don't trust them!

Take time to adjust the height of the mike so you don't have to lean into it, or have it covering your face.

The general rule is to stand at least six to eight inches away from it. Be aware that public address mikes are not of very high quality and are very different from the mikes you see used by rock stars; getting too close can cause feedback. Instead, notice the way "on-the-scene" reporters use their mikes. This is more like the distance you want. A lavaliere mike, the kind you clip on or hang around your neck, will pick up your voice without forcing you to bend your head down.

If there's feedback, hold the mike further from your mouth. Check to see that no speakers are pointed at the podium. Ask your host for assistance if the problem persists.

Make your host look good

Once again, good manners and good marketing go hand in hand. At the very start of your event, make sure you thank and compliment your host and staff. Make 'em love you.

Authors who sell a lot of their own books — a how-to book sold at seminars, for instance — and who are appearing at a store must never try to steal customers from their host. It is considered rankest heresy for the author to offer even a multiple copy price lower than the store can match.

Be prepared for autographing

Your hands and fingernails are buffed to perfection, right? Bring a pen you like — two actually, what if one runs dry? — a pen that lets you write a smooth bold signature. As a security precaution, don't use the same signature you use to sign your checks, though.

Choose which page to sign. Traditionally, authors have signed the title page, but depending on the layout, this page may not have room for your signature and an inscription. If your book has a half-title page — a page prior to the title page, containing just the title, no author's name or publisher, or else a small piece of art — this would be a good place. Or a blank page facing the title page. Leave the inside flyleaf for personal inscriptions from giver to recipient.

Unless you have a very long line, do more than just sign. The goal is to create an attractive note in the book. Beware of smears and smudges. If your book is printed on slick paper, as many books with photographs or color illustrations are, the paper is not absorptive, and ink dries much more slowly. As smearing can be a serious problem, you may wish to bring a small blotter. An archival quality pen such as the Zig Millenium will also do the trick. The ink is fast-drying, and doesn't bleed or fade (ask at art supply stores). Or try a photographic pen from a camera supply store.

Some authors add an artistic touch. For his *Book of the Dead Man* series, poet Marvin Bell found a stamp of a skeleton. Armed with a pad of green ink, he stamped the image beside his signature for a very arresting look. Of course he ended up green halfway to his elbows and had to take special care not to smear, but it made for a unique personalized inscription.

Authors of children's books might find stamps a good way to make the autographing process more inter-active. Perhaps you could offer to also stamp the hands of any kids buying the book. With their parent's permission, of course, and using washable non-toxic ink in these litigious times.

Decide ahead of time what you're going to use for a generic inscription. Do ad-lib inscriptions as you please and time permits, but you need a pre-planned piece. It should be something short and punchy from the book, or about it. Personalize the inscription with a name: if there is any doubt of the spelling, check and double-check.

An angry book buyer is a fearsome thing. In his book *Roads,* Larry McMurtry told the story of his worst-ever book signing. It began with a dim hall and a sullen after-dinner audience that refused to give up a single spark of energy. No table had been set up for signing, so McMurtry was forced to balance books on his lap with people crowding around his chair. The ultimate depth of that abysmal evening came when an elderly lady took a drunken swat at him with her purse. " 'You didn't hardly write nothin' in my book,' she said...." Plan your inscription in advance and beware of big purses.

Always offer to autograph any unsold stock the bookstore may have on hand. This gives the bookseller an additional selling tool — "An Autographed Copy" — and they are less likely to return it for credit.

Make a graceful exit

Once you've done everything you came for, and the last potential customer has been offered a chance to buy, collect yourself with a minimum of fuss and disruption. Just because your presentation is over doesn't mean that your host isn't still trying to conduct business.

NAKED AT THE PODIUM

Evening events may coincide with the store's closing hours. If your audience is too enthusiastic to let go, don't keep the staff hanging around, move the party to a coffee shop or tavern nearby. The staff will need half an hour to put the store to bed from the moment you and your last followers walk out the door.

Don't draw out your good-byes. Make sure you've got all names and relevant information; you've checked out with your host; and you've said a last word to any sales people who seemed attracted to your book. And don't forget, if you were offered a fee to speak, as for a lecture, be sure to collect it on your way out.

Follow-up afterwards

Send thank-you notes. This is not just good manners, it makes marketing sense. You want them to like you and invite you back to sell your next book. So send a note to the organization or store where you appeared, thanking them for their efforts and complimenting them where appropriate, *by name*. Include copies of the photograph you had taken at your appearance, if you were able to make that happen — a copy for each staff member in the shot. This will help them remember you, place the face and the name together. In fact, if you have an inexpensive scanner and color printer, you can create very effective post-marketing tools. On the back of your copy, note the name of the store or group, the date, the title of the book you were pushing, and the names of the staff members shown. File the photo away for your next book.

Be sure to ask for any feedback on your performance, what they liked, or thought needed improvement. This is another opportunity to connect with the staff, and give them a feeling of personal investment in you and your book.

Debrief with a friend or spouse, or simply with yourself, after each performance. How many people attended, and how many sales did you have? Make notes while your memory is fresh about what worked and what didn't, any feedback you got, or ideas you had for change and improvement.

Now is the time to have a glass of wine and celebrate. You've done everything you can to be successful. The Duc de la Rochefoucauld would be proud of you.

CHAPTER ELEVEN

Audience Members with Disabilities

Luanne LaLonde

Who come with varied tongues, but hearts the same...,
Oliver Wendell Holmes

Get a grip, Jeffrey. He probably didn't realize you were an elephant when he told that last joke!
With apologies to Gary Larson

Approach

Nothing turns off a person with a disability more than being singled out, unless it's being ignored. There are some times when you need to address or accommodate someone in a different manner, but for the most part there's no reason to point out the obvious.

If you engage the audience with lots of eye contact, don't go sweeping past someone in the audience who has a disability as if he isn't there. Even if that person is blind. On the other hand, things like sign language interpretation or someone who's unable to control his movements can be distracting. So try not to fixate on a person with a disability or on the accommodation that's been made.

Every culture has its own form of introduction and congratulations. In the U.S., we shake hands. If the setting suggests a handshake, offer your hand to someone with a physical disability even if you aren't sure he or she can take it. If not, it will only take one or two seconds to determine that and if it seems both of you would be comfortable just extend your hand for a brief touch on the forearm, for instance. In the case of a person who is blind or has a visual impairment, reach out and take his hand to shake it.

Terminology

We're so tuned into political correctness nowadays that being suddenly confronted by the need to address someone with a disability can be more uncomfortable than it should be. Except for being aware of what might be offensive, such terms as "cripple" or "retarded," you shouldn't be uncomfortable or intimidated.

The rule of thumb is *do not label.* Referring to someone by defining that person by his disability, you color not only others' perceptions but also what you're conveying to that person about your own opinions and prejudices. You would never call upon someone in the audience by saying, "the fat guy in the third row." Don't be tempted to address someone in a wheelchair by referring to his chair, or a blind person by referring to his disability.

The best way to conduct Q & A, no matter what

the situation, is not to nod or point at people, but to call upon "the lady in yellow in the middle of the fourth row," or "the gentleman in blue at the back." A blind person knows what he's wearing and approximately where he's seated in the room so that's enough to go on.

References in everyday language

It's a hearing, seeing, mobile world and no one expects you to change how you, personally, fit into it. There's no need for heightened awareness of the phrases you use. Blind people say, "See you later," and, "I've got to watch the time." Someone with a physical disability shouldn't take offense if you use the phrase, "Put yourself in my shoes." A person in a wheelchair may invite you to, "walk down to the restaurant with us." If nothing else, that's just a way to make it clear you'll be walking somewhere and not taking a cab or bus.

Deaf or hard of hearing

Whether or not a person is totally deaf, he/she relies much more on body language and facial expression than a hearing person. It's necessary to address the audience head-on and not with the head down or with no eye contact. Keep the microphone clear of your face.

If an audience member is using a sign language interpreter, whether provided for the event or just along as a friend, ask the interpreter beforehand, if you have a chance, to let you know if you're going too fast. Tell him or her to go ahead and interrupt you or give you a signal if you're speaking too fast or the topic isn't clear. You do *not* have to change how you present yourself or your work: that's for the interpreter to do and the deaf person will take other cues from you and the audience. (For example: don't "over-explain" a joke because you think a deaf person needs more description to get it. He'll get the gist of it and will get other cues from the audience.) Beyond that, there's very little you need to know about sign language interpretation, so just relax. It's not about you!

Tom Robbins, an author whose playful use of language delights and challenges his readers, appeared at the Bumbershoot Literary Festival in Seattle, a few years back. He read the opening sentence from his short story, *Moonlight Whoopee Cushion Sonata,* "The witch girl who lives by the bend in the river is said to keep a fart in a bottle." Then he paused while the laughter subsided, and eyed the sign language interpreter. "I hope they've got you on danger pay tonight," said Robbins. "You're going to earn it." It was a wonderful inclusive moment, and set the tone for the rest of the reading. And at the end, the interpreter got an ovation from the entire audience.

In fact, your audience may find the sign language interpreter so fascinating, you have to work extra hard to direct their attention back to you!

Just as people with poor vision sit closer to the stage or screen in order to catch the visual effects of a reading or presentation, people with hearing disabilities will most likely sit in that part of the room which best fits their needs. If they need an interpreter they'll sit where there's enough light to see the interpreter, and they'll also want to sit where they're in line to see both the interpreter and you at the same time. If necessary, this is one time when you may offer to help if it seems such a spot isn't readily available in the audience. You or your host should ask someone in the audience to move to make room, and/or you'll need to move from your original position at the front to help rectify the situation.

Q & A

During Q & A you should always repeat the question. If someone has seated himself in the audience to best listen to you he may not be able to hear people in other parts of the room. This is true for just about anyone, not just someone with a disability. For instance, one side of the room might be closer to the street or to another room where there is noise, and you have to take that extra noise into consideration.

Repeating the question is an excellent habit to get into anyway, to ensure you haven't misinterpreted the original question yourself (see Chapter Nine). Rather than prattling on about something that wasn't asked, you can make sure you're addressing the question correctly.

If someone speaks slowly or with a speech impediment, use common sense and courtesy. Don't interrupt. If you're not sure you understood everything correctly just paraphrase what you heard. Remember that the question is most likely related to your presentation and that should help put what you're hearing in context. It might take a couple of times to get it right.

People with cerebral palsy, multiple sclerosis, or Parkinson's disease often have difficulty speaking. Many such disabilities are acquired later in life (think of

Muhammad Ali and Michael J. Fox). It is unbelievably frustrating to have lost the ability to communicate. Stop for a second and think: this could happen to you. Don't be condescending. The audience will take their cue from you, and if you don't show impatience they probably won't either.

Blind or visually impaired

If you're doing a reading and want to engage the audience by prepping them for what's seen and imagined, think of what you'd have to do or say if you were conducting the session over the telephone. Or maybe you've got a parent with poor vision. What's important? Present yourself and the topic in a colorful, meaningful way.

Or, you could probably close your eyes and imagine what you see or what you want them to see. Pretend you're blind and have to convey what you see and what's in your imagination. When you're in front of an audience, if you keep these things in mind you'll be accommodating anyone out there with a visual impairment.

If your reading or presentation includes visual text, you should read that content aloud as appropriate. If you're doing a slide presentation, read the points on each slide before launching into the rhetoric. It helps focus everyone, plus it brings home those points you thought were so important they warranted being written down.

If you're giving out handouts, give them to everyone, regardless of whether you think they can see or hold the item.

If you want a show of hands from the audience, ask for it. Don't just silently raise your hand indicating you want that type of response from people.

If you're playing a character — and if you're good at it — entertainment is a great way to hurdle that invisible barrier between people with disabilities and those without and puts everyone (including yourself) at ease.

If you use your hands and a lot of facial expressions you're not going to be able to do much about it. In some cases such things can be distracting to audience members. But oftentimes they help engage the audience, especially if you're doing something humorous. If you've got people with visual impairments in the audience, don't worry about it, just keep in mind that you shouldn't try to convey lots of material with hand and/or facial expressions.

If you're using props, describe them briefly then get on with it. But the more information about the setting you can work into your dialogue the better you'll be. "I come to you on this empty stage, lit only by a spotlight, carrying only a Starbucks supremo grande double latte, a 40-year-old woman with this message to bear." You get the idea. You'll be surprised how much this helps any audience: *you* get to create even the most simple setting, rather than just leaving it up to them.

But no matter how awkward you may feel, press on with your presentation. It can't be worse than my Tokyo nightmare.

A blind man describes your elephant

In 1998 I was one of the principal members of Microsoft's Accessibility Technology Group. At a meeting of an association of the deaf in Tokyo I was to give a demonstration of the company's new closed captioning technology.

Upon arriving, to my dismay I learned the English/Japanese translator had become ill at the last minute and we had no language interpreter.

One of my teammate's friends, Masafumi Nakane (Max), happened to be present. Since he speaks fluent English and works in the software industry, he was enlisted to do the language translation. The problem was Max is blind.

Thus I had to do a software demonstration in English which would be translated by a blind man into Japanese, for a Japanese audience that would *actually* get their info from the sign language interpreters and open-captioning typists who were listening only to the blind man's version of what I was saying.

Max had to listen to every single word I said in order to explain a complex visual technology he didn't totally understand — without knowing the specific elements I was showing to the deaf crowd. Yet the audience could see what I was doing, so the descriptions I was giving Max were much more detailed than necessary because he had to figure out the technology on the fly.

This public speaker's nightmare lasted an hour, and then we did Q & A. It was amazing! From the audience's questions (which went through this process in reverse) I realized they really did understand the technology and how it worked. Max had done an unbelievable job describing something he could not see.

I received polite applause at the end. Max got a standing ovation.

CHAPTER TWELVE

What If NOBODY Shows Up?

...I risked everything for adventure; I did my best, and was over-thrown.... I did not lose, nor could I lose my integrity, and I can still fulfill my promise.
        Don Quixote, Miguel de Cervantes Saavedra

It's my party and I'll cry if I want to!
        Leslie Gore

This allegedly happened to a poet and photographer now deceased. A nice man and a good poet. One can't name him, because it would be cruel and because we can't prove it. Maybe it's an urban legend. Anyway, call him Alfred.

Alfred was said in the story to be a graduate of an Ivy League school and so was honored to be invited back to read there. When he arrived at the university, his host greeted him apologetically and explained that he had an important meeting to fly to that very day, in Boston. He'd had no luck in changing it and therefore would have to leave right after introducing Alfred. He would have a cab waiting to race him to the airport. Alfred said no problem, he fully understood.

When they arrived at the reading room, only two people were there so far: two young men sitting next to one another toward the front. Five minutes passed. Alfred's host apologized again and said he couldn't wait for others to show up but had to introduce him on time and catch his cab. "No problem," said Alfred, who understood.

The man gave Alfred a nice introduction, wished him well and exited toward his cab. Alfred stood up and began to read his first poem. One of the two students raised a hand and said, "Excuse me. Are you going to be doing that long? My friend and I wanted to study in here."

Is that your biggest fear? That you'll give a party and nobody will come? It lends a certain urgency to your advertising efforts. This is why you sift your mind for people you know to invite for every presentation. But suppose it happens? Is this the end of the world? Is it time to reach for your asp?

Major disaster or minor catastrophe?

Let's consider a minute. We're not talking about a sit-and-sign at the mall, with people drifting past your table talking on cell phones, looking for fudge or just cruising. What did you expect? You just have to sit. And if by "nobody came," you mean only a handful showed up and you were expecting a screaming throng — get out of here. If there are ten people in a hall for three hundred and you've been hired to speak, you speak.

Invite the ten people to move down to the good seats, make a joke about the situation, and give them your very best show. If you've got two people in a bookstore, turn your presentation into more of a conversation. Sending two people out the door with your book and a real excitement about reading it, you're creating hard-core fans who will start word-of-mouth.

But what if you go to make a presentation and nobody comes? We mean *nobody.* Even your spouse couldn't make it that day.

Alfred's story is absolutely the worst that can happen to a writer. First, because he entered the situation with such high expectations, which were completely dashed. Second, because he got no chance to reach so much as a single reader. Third, because he had no host or staff to commiserate with. And last, because he didn't even have a ride home.

You are unlikely to meet with such a high-caliber disaster. Just a little minor catastrophe now and then. This is how you deal with it.

Handling the shock

If you're all warmed up and ready to go, and there's no go, you'll have a lot of performance energy pent up inside that's ready to go play. This unexpended energy can back up on you, emotionally. Hurt, anger and embarrassment are the most common reactions, and you're likely to be feeling those anyway. Take some deep, calming breaths. You've got to play this professionally. Save your emotions until you get home. We'll deal with them later.

This is the moment when you really have to focus on the fact that your hosts are on your side, and that they're trying their best for you. If this is a lost opportunity for you, it is also a lost opportunity for them; they were counting on a crowd, on book sales, on a boost for their organization, too. So you're not the only one who has gotten a thumb in the eye. The thing is, if you want to be a career writer, you will have future books to sell. You can't afford to blow off a connection because your pride is hurt. You may decide not to deal with them again, but that's a decision to be made only after a forty-eight hour cooling-off period. Meanwhile, consult with your host. Be calm and pleasant, even if you want to make lots and lots of noise.

> PK: For those of you with a philosophical bent, my brother the engineer recommends Aristotle on the Archer. It's worth meditating on at moments like this. For the rest of us with short attention spans, the thought is that even an arrow that misses the target is useful. The wise archer observes every flight, and so can learn more about his bow, his aim, and how to judge shooting conditions from even the wildest miss.

Besides, your name may have been in the newspaper, in the store's mailings, newsletter and signs. Advertising people will tell you it takes time and repetition to develop brand-name familiarity. You'd have to pay big bucks to buy opportunities you've just had, even if they didn't bring results *this time.*

Making bad bananas into banana bread

When it's finally obvious that no one is coming, consult with your host, and see what they would like you to do. Conduct a brief, positive post-mortem. No guilt trips, no heavy sighs. You want their take on what happened, so you can learn from it. Was your appearance scheduled opposite some big community event? Were there problems with your mailings? Parking, a snowstorm, earthquake or riots in the streets? What does the staff think?

If it's a bookstore appearance, always offer to autograph their stock. And then, ask if you can pitch your book to the staff, either a couple of minutes together in a group, if the place isn't crowded, or one by one. Give them your very best fall-in-love-with-my-book lines. Be sure you tell them:

> Who this book is for.
> What made you write it.
> What's the best thing about it.

And tell them a curious or funny or touching story about something in the book and how it came to be there. Booksellers need a whole set of hooks and lures to catch customers. This is a great opportunity for you to provide them.

You are winding these folks up to hand-sell your book for days, weeks, months after you've gone home. You want them to love you and want to do this for you. Groveling and pleading won't do, and you can't afford bribery. Summon your own great enthusiasm about your book. Remember why you wrote it, and why you love it.

PK: Take a moment to look at your booksellers. See them as people. I learned a valuable lesson once, traveling in Spain. When I first landed in Madrid I found that with my phrase book Spanish I would assemble my requests in my head before going into a store, march up to the counter and say, "I wish to purchase two of these and three of those." And the clerk would invariably respond, "Hello. How are you today?" And because I was so tuned in to what I wanted, I would have to scramble together a polite answer. We had to greet each other first, and then we would get on to the business of what it was I wanted to purchase. By the end of the trip my manners were much improved.

When feeling stressed or dislocated, we focus on our own needs and don't relate well to others. Right now you need to relate well with these particular individuals. Booksellers love books. They should be straw to your flame if you can convey your enthusiasm. And this is a time when having a photo taken with the staff would really be good, so you can send copies with your thank-you note.

Maintaining your morale

Once you have packed up and removed yourself from the scene, go someplace relatively protected where you can be alone to begin venting your internal steam. Tears, yells, songs, curses, prayers and laughter may be combined as needed.

Realize that you have taken a blow in a very tender spot. Rally yourself, and shake off the effects of the blow. Do something physical to burn off your pent-up performance energy. Go for a walk, but not in the rain — unless you like the rain. Do nothing that mortifies the flesh. You're looking for a way to release those positive exercise endorphins.

Give yourself a treat before the day is out. Nothing big or fancy, just a little something to make you feel as if you got a present. A spoonful of sugar helps the medicine go down.

Write a script to describe the event. You'll be asked about it, what will you say? The script should go something like, "The attendance was disappointing, but I got the chance to pitch to the staff, and I really think I connected with them. Oh, and they said they thought the World Series game that afternoon was tough competition for my book on sports trivia." Acknowledge the reality without wallowing in it, then move directly to the positives and spend your words there.

It is human nature to take rejection to heart, and to tell and retell our misery, seeking consolation. The problem is that saying the words out loud becomes like a mantra, a chant to meditate on. A meditation on misery will be as useful as going out to the garden to eat worms. So write your script and accentuate the positives. That's your story, and you're sticking to it.

For the next three days, take twenty minutes a day and go back and read your favorite parts in the book. Feed your enthusiasm. On the fourth day, do a full rehearsal of the presentation you didn't get to make. Think about how to make it even better next time.

It's your party, you can cry if you want to; but target practice makes more sense.

CHAPTER THIRTEEN

Closing the Sale

When I get a little money, I buy books;
and if there is any left over, I buy food and clothes.

Erasmus

You've got your show on its feet, and you're taking it on the road. You've only got one thing left to do, and it is the very hardest thing of all: you've got to sell your book.

Closing the sale is where we freeze up, as authors. For many of us, a problem arises when we cross the line from telling people about our book, and why it's wonderful, and move into saying, "please buy my book."

PK: Recently I attended a presentation by a local author. She did an excellent job using visual aids and artifacts central to the book. She didn't try for a fancy song and dance, she let her own style and charm work for her, and the audience was truly engaged. When the Q & A session ended, she thanked everyone for coming and got a nice round of applause. Then the audience stood up as if to leave. Fortunately, I was standing at the back of the room, between them and the door. I raised my voice and said, "Books are available at the front table. The author will be happy to autograph your copy." And two-thirds of them dutifully formed into line to buy one.

How many copies would have been sold had I not intervened, I can't say. But the key here is that they weren't asked to buy. When they were, they responded. The author had been waiting for the host to say something, the host had been waylaid at the crucial moment and wasn't ready to speak, and the moment might have been missed.

This problem is usually a branch of the self-promotion problem. Raleigh Pinskey, the author and public relations maven, suggests that childhood messages such as "Don't brag," "What makes you think you have anything to offer?" and "Don't talk to strangers," make us reluctant to put ourselves forward. We're shy about asking for what we want. For some writers, the issue may be that we're crossing the line from art into commerce.

Whatever the reason, this reluctance is a problem that must be solved before we go out on the road. The whole reason for us to put on a show is to sell our books. Pulling up short at the end is not an option. What we have to do is plan a way to get over our hurdle.

The first thing to do is give a great presentation. If you can make your audience laugh or cry or learn something, you've got one leg over already. A good presentation engages your audience, makes them identify with you and develops their curiosity about your book. You're off to a running start because the people who come to hear you have already expressed an interest. They are willing to be sold. Now you've got to close the sale.

Have you ever seen Ron Popeil, or any of the other really successful infomercial masters? These folks are super salesmen, and if you ever watch the way they pitch their wares, you'll see they have a trick they use that works every time. They make the product into the star of the show. They don't shine the spotlight on themselves; they shine it on the Tomato Shredder or the Thigh Wonker, or whatever they are selling.

Don't flash the book at the audience every few seconds, as if you're conducting subliminal advertising. You don't have to work quite so hard; your book is more attractive than any Thigh Wonker ever invented. But you do need to hold it up periodically, and especially at the end of your show. You do need to focus the audience on the idea that if they enjoyed your presentation, all this and more is waiting for them right between the covers of this little book, absolutely guaranteed!

The easiest way is to write an exit line for yourself. That way you can take the time to think about it and polish it the way you would an opening sentence. Get it right so you feel good about it. You don't have to be blatant and hit them over the head with it. You are writing advertising copy again, so keep it short and punchy.

Self-deprecating humor may be your best device. Whatever approach you choose, you want to have a windup line. Something that reconnects you with them, and summarizes the event and says, "I hope you'll buy my book. I'll be glad to autograph it for you." If your host says it also, the audience has been asked to buy twice, and repetition is good salesmanship. If your host has forgotten, or been waylaid, at least the request has been made.

We're not talking about cold-calling, going door-to-door selling vacuum cleaners or magazine subscriptions. These people came out to see you. They are interested. They want to get hooked. You're doing them a favor. After all, food just rots. They should buy books. Your books.

CHAPTER FOURTEEN

Places, Everybody

...this really cannot be called courage
until you have swallowed it.

The Wizard of Oz

Now you're ready to become the voice of your book in the marketplace. That's what all those writers are doing at your local bookstore or lecture series. They're being a voice for their books. You're just doing the same thing that Terry McMillan does, or Dave Barry.

To be the living voice for your book you have to sell yourself to your audience. Now you're ready to do that. You've learned how to prepare your material and yourself to connect with people. Book sales will follow.

You can:

Enchant your audience.

Make bookstores love you.

Cure your jitters.

Prepare like a pro.

Use your voice and body.

Become your characters.

Survive unusual venues.

As a published writer, you don't plan to be a one-book wonder. You want to write more books and have them published, too. And the fact of the matter is, you have to be able to sell your book, if you want to be paid to write another. The writing and the selling are two sides of the same coin.

Do you know how the Cowardly Lion became the bravest beast in Oz? The Wizard poured the contents of a square green bottle into a green-gold bowl. When he set the bowl before the Lion, he told him that "...courage is always inside one; so that this really cannot be called courage until you've swallowed it. Therefore I advise you to drink it as soon as possible." The Lion drank till the dish was empty.

Let's go put on a show.

BIBLIOGRAPHY

Blanco, Jodee. THE COMPLETE GUIDE TO BOOK PUBLICITY. New York: Allworth Press, 2000.

Cole, David. THE COMPLETE GUIDE TO BOOK MARKETING. New York: Allworth Press, 1999.

Fiertag, Joe and Mary Carmen Cupito. THE WRITER'S MARKET COMPANION. Cincinnati: Writer's Digest Books, 2000.

Hoff, Ron. I CAN SEE YOU NAKED. Kansas City: Andrews and McMeel Publishing, 1992.

Kremer, John. 1001 WAYS TO MARKET YOUR BOOKS: FOR AUTHORS AND PUBLISHERS. Fairfield: Open Horizons, 1998 (5th edition).

LITERARY MARKET PLACE. New Providence: R. R. Bowker, 2000.

Marconi, Joe. THE COMPLETE GUIDE TO PUBLICITY: Maximum Visibility for Your Product, Service or Organization. Lincolnwood: NTC Business Books, 1999.

Poynter, Dan. SELF-PUBLISHING MANUAL, THE: How To Write, Print And Sell Your Own Book. Santa Barbara: Para Publishing, 2000 (12th Edition).

Rein, Irving, Philip Kotler, and Martin Stoller. HIGH VISIBILITY: The Making and Marketing of Professionals into Celebrities. Lincolnwood: NTC Business Books, 1997.

Ristad, Eloise. A SOPRANO ON HER HEAD: Right-Side-Up Reflections On Life And Other Performances. Moab: Real People Press, 1982.

Ross, Tom & Marilyn. THE COMPLETE GUIDE TO SELF PUBLISHING. Cincinnati: Writer's Digest Books, 1994 (3rd edition).

Sedge, Michael. MARKETING STRATEGIES FOR WRITERS. New York: Allworth Press, 1999.

NOTES

NOTES

NOTES

74th Street Productions

...and to think I found it on 74th Street!

An independent publishing company
specializing in Shakespeare, theatre
and the literary arts.

QUICK ORDER FORM

Web site: **www.74thstreet.com**
Toll free phone: **888-781-1447**
Fax orders (send this form): **888-781-1447**
E-mail orders: **info@74thstreet.com**
Postal orders: **74th Street Productions**
350 N. 74th Street
Seattle, WA 98103, USA

SEND TO: (We will not sell/provide your name to any other organization.)

NAME _____

ADDRESS _____

CITY/STATE/ZIP _____

COUNTRY _____

PHONE/AREA CODE (   ) _____

E-MAIL _____

Please send _____ **copies of** *NAKED AT THE PODIUM:*
THE WRITER'S GUIDE TO SUCCESSFUL READINGS.

_____ @ $15.95 USA ($22 CAN) = _____

Sales tax: add 8.8% to orders shipped to WA state = _____

For shipping by priority mail:

US: $5 first book and $1.50 ea. addl. book = _____

International: $9 first book and $3 ea. addl. book = _____

☐ **CHECK ENCLOSED FOR $** _____ **or**

CREDIT CARD: ☐ **VISA**   ☐ **MASTERCARD**   **EXP DATE:** _____ / _____

CARD #: _____

NAME ON CARD: _____

BILLING ADDRESS: *(if different from shipping address)* (please print)

_____

_____

ATTENTION COLLEGES AND UNIVERSITIES, CORPORATIONS, AND PROFESSIONAL ORGANIZATIONS: Quantity discounts are available on bulk purchases of this book for educational training purposes, fund raising, or gift giving.

74th Street Productions

...and to think I found it on 74th Street!

An independent publishing company
specializing in Shakespeare, theatre
and the literary arts.

QUICK ORDER FORM

Web site:	**www.74thstreet.com**
Toll free phone:	**888-781-1447**
Fax orders (send this form):	**888-781-1447**
E-mail orders:	**info@74thstreet.com**
Postal orders:	**74th Street Productions**
	350 N. 74th Street
	Seattle, WA 98103, USA

SEND TO: (We will not sell/provide your name to any other organization.)

NAME _____

ADDRESS _____

CITY/STATE/ZIP _____

COUNTRY _____

PHONE/AREA CODE (   ) _____

E-MAIL _____

Please send _____ copies of *NAKED AT THE PODIUM:*
THE WRITER'S GUIDE TO SUCCESSFUL READINGS.

_____ @ $15.95 USA ($22 CAN) = _____

Sales tax: add 8.8% to orders shipped to WA state = _____

For shipping by priority mail:

US: $5 first book and $1.50 ea. addl. book = _____

International: $9 first book and $3 ea. addl. book = _____

☐ **CHECK ENCLOSED FOR $** _____ **or**

CREDIT CARD: ☐ **VISA** ☐ **MASTERCARD** **EXP DATE:** _____ / _____

CARD #: _____

NAME ON CARD: _____

BILLING ADDRESS: *(if different from shipping address)* (please print)

_____

_____

ATTENTION COLLEGES AND UNIVERSITIES, CORPORATIONS, AND PROFESSIONAL ORGANIZATIONS: Quantity discounts are available on bulk purchases of this book for educational training purposes, fund raising, or gift giving.

74th Street Productions

...and to think I found it on 74th Street!

An independent publishing company
specializing in Shakespeare, theatre
and the literary arts.

QUICK ORDER FORM

Web site: **www.74thstreet.com**
Toll free phone: **888-781-1447**
Fax orders (send this form): **888-781-1447**
E-mail orders: **info@74thstreet.com**
Postal orders: **74th Street Productions**
                          350 N. 74th Street
                          Seattle, WA 98103, USA

SEND TO: (We will not sell/provide your name to any other organization.)

NAME _____

ADDRESS _____

CITY/STATE/ZIP _____

COUNTRY _____

PHONE/AREA CODE ( ) _____

E-MAIL _____

Please send _____ **copies of *NAKED AT THE PODIUM:***
THE WRITER'S GUIDE TO SUCCESSFUL READINGS.

    _____ @ $15.95 USA ($22 CAN) = _____

    Sales tax: add 8.8% to orders shipped to WA state = _____

For shipping by priority mail:

    US: $5 first book and $1.50 ea. addl. book = _____

    International: $9 first book and $3 ea. addl. book = _____

☐ **CHECK ENCLOSED FOR $** _____ **or**

CREDIT CARD: ☐ **VISA** ☐ **MASTERCARD**   **EXP DATE:** _____ / _____

CARD #: _____

NAME ON CARD: _____

BILLING ADDRESS: *(if different from shipping address)* (please print)

_____

_____

ATTENTION COLLEGES AND UNIVERSITIES, CORPORATIONS, AND PROFESSIONAL ORGANIZATIONS: Quantity discounts are available on bulk purchases of this book for educational training purposes, fund raising, or gift giving.

74th Street Productions

...and to think I found it on 74ᵗʰ Street!

An independent publishing company
specializing in Shakespeare, theatre
and the literary arts.

QUICK ORDER FORM

Web site: **www.74thstreet.com**
Toll free phone: **888-781-1447**
Fax orders (send this form): **888-781-1447**
E-mail orders: **info@74thstreet.com**
Postal orders: **74th Street Productions**
350 N. 74th Street
Seattle, WA 98103, USA

SEND TO: (We will not sell/provide your name to any other organization.)

NAME _____

ADDRESS _____

CITY/STATE/ZIP _____

COUNTRY _____

PHONE/AREA CODE (   ) _____

E-MAIL _____

Please send _____ copies of *NAKED AT THE PODIUM:*
THE WRITER'S GUIDE TO SUCCESSFUL READINGS.

_____ @ $15.95 USA ($22 CAN) = _____

Sales tax: add 8.8% to orders shipped to WA state = _____

For shipping by priority mail:

US: $5 first book and $1.50 ea addl book = _____

International: $9 first book and $3 ea addl book = _____

☐ **CHECK ENCLOSED FOR $** _____ **or**

CREDIT CARD: ☐ **VISA** ☐ **MASTERCARD**   **EXP DATE:** _____ / _____

CARD #: _____

NAME ON CARD: _____

BILLING ADDRESS: *(if different from shipping address)* (please print)

_____

_____

ATTENTION COLLEGES AND UNIVERSITIES, CORPORATIONS, AND PROFESSIONAL ORGANIZATIONS: Quantity discounts are available on bulk purchases of this book for educational training purposes, fund raising, or gift giving.